# The Struggle
# for Freedom

Library of
AFRICAN-AMERICAN HISTORY

# The Struggle for Freedom

## AFRICAN-AMERICAN SLAVE RESISTANCE

**DENNIS WEPMAN**

Facts On File, Inc.

AN INFOBASE HOLDINGS COMPANY

The author would like to acknowledge the courtesy and help of the Sullivan County Community College Library staff, and to give his special thanks to his editors, Nicole Bowen and Emily Ross, and his agent, Ivy Fischer Stone.

**The Struggle for Freedom: African-American Slave Resistance**

Facts On File, Inc.
11 Penn Plaza
New York NY 10001

**Library of Congress Cataloging-in-Publication Data**

Wepman, Dennis.
   The struggle for freedom : African-American slave resistance /
Dennis Wepman
      p. cm. — (Library of African-American history)
   Includes bibliographical references and index.
   ISBN 0-8160-3270-X (alk. paper)
   1. Slavery—United States—Insurrections, etc.—Juvenile literature.
   2. Slavery—Insurrections, etc.—Juvenile literature.   3. Fugitive slaves—United
States—Juvenile literature.   4. Slaves—United States—Social conditions—
Juvenile literature.   I. Title.   II. Series.
E447.W46   1996
306.3'62—dc20                                                                    95-34557

Text design by Catherine Rincon Hyman
Cover design by Nora Wertz

This book is printed on acid-free paper

Printed in the United States of America

MP FOF 10 9 8 7 6 5 4 3 2 1

# Contents

# How It Began:
# The Roots of
# U.S. Slavery

No one argues today about whether slavery is right or wrong, but until fairly recently it was one of the most controversial subjects in the Western world. Some people considered slavery a necessary and just social system, profitable to both slave and master. Others believed it was morally wrong and contrary to God's will. Americans were deeply divided about slavery from its first appearance in the New World during the 16th century. By the mid-19th century the issue nearly tore the country apart.

Slavery did not originate in America. The practice of people owning other people as property has deep historical roots and has existed in various forms in virtually every part of the world.

## Slavery in Ancient Times

There are records of slavery dating back 6,000 years to the written laws of Sumer, a part of ancient Babylonia, now within Iraq. The Code of Hammurabi, king of Babylonia in the 18th century B.C., contains rules governing the practice. The Hebrews were slaves in ancient Egypt, and the Bible reports that they themselves held slaves before and after their own period of bondage. The Greeks were dependent on slavery as early as 1200 B.C., and the philosopher Plato described the ideal society as one in which all labor would be done by slaves. At the height of the Greek Empire, 5 million free Greeks were supported by the labor of 12 million slaves.

In ancient Persia, slaves were bred like cattle and were bought and sold like any other commodity. In other societies, slavery was a common method of paying debts—a man could sell himself or his children when he owed money. Criminals provided another source of slaves: enslavement, for a fixed period or for life, was a

> The state of slavery
>
> is in its own nature bad.
>
> It is neither useful to the master
>
> nor to the slave; not to the slave,
>
> because he can do nothing
>
> through a motive of virtue;
>
> nor to the master, because by
>
> having an unlimited authority
>
> over his slaves he insensibly
>
> accustoms himself to the want of
>
> all moral virtues and thence
>
> becomes fiery, hasty, severe,
>
> choleric, voluptuous and cruel.
>
> ◆
>
> Charles, baron de Montesquieu,
> The Spirit of Laws (1748)

punishment for breaking the law in many parts of Africa, Europe, and the Near East. But war furnished the largest source of slaves in ancient times. Conquered people were considered lawful loot, and captured men and women were sold as laborers in many parts of the world. The Roman armies supplied their empire with the largest slave population of ancient times. In 167 B.C., the Roman historian Plutarch described a market where 150,000 slaves were sold in one day.

The Roman slave system ranks as one of the cruelest in history. Slaves had almost no rights. They could not marry. Often they were chained together in work gangs. The old and sick were left on an island in the Tiber River to die of hunger. It was lawful for masters to kill their slaves; history records a Roman named Vedius Pollio who entertained his dinner guests by throwing slaves to man-eating fish he kept in a pool for just that purpose.

Yet Roman slavery had some relatively humane features. It was possible for slaves to earn money to buy their freedom, and capable slaves could be appointed to positions of power in the government. In the first century A.D., Roman laws were changed to improve conditions slightly. Owners lost the right to kill their slaves or treat them with excessive cruelty.

Despite the opportunities they had to better their lot, Roman slaves seldom submitted willingly. In some areas they so outnumbered free citizens that rebellion was inevitable. A slave uprising occurred in Sicily in 134 B.C., and another one 30 years later, but both were easily suppressed. In 73 B.C., however, the third and most important rebellion nearly succeeded in toppling the empire.

Spartacus was a Roman slave captured in Thrace, a warlike nation that occupied parts of what are now Greece, Bulgaria, and Turkey. A powerful fighter, he was sold as a gladiator and forced to fight publicly to the death with other gladiators, and even with wild beasts. Determined to become a free man, he escaped in 73 B.C., and then inspired other

# Proslavery Thought

The arguments against slavery, which seem so self-evident to us today, were not always universally recognized. During the first centuries of American history, the institution had many respectable defenders, including scholars, statesmen, and clergymen. A large body of literature exists that attempts to prove slavery morally right and good for both master and slave.

Advocates justified slavery as workable and necessary, pointing to the historical fact that all great civilizations had depended on it. Such social philosophers as George Fitzhugh wrote in the 1850s that the economic laws of world trade made slavery essential, and that it was better than the "wage slavery" of Northern industrial capitalism. A Southern slave owner himself, Fitzhugh believed that slavery was a benevolent arrangement that protected the slave from unemployment and want.

John C. Calhoun, vice president under John Quincy Adams and Andrew Jackson, defended slavery with a political argument; without it, he maintained, the Union would dissolve and the nation would fall.

runaway slaves to join him in his fight against Rome. Some reports estimate that his army numbered as many as 90,000. Within a year they dominated much of southern Italy. Spartacus defeated the Romans in seven major battles, but after two years his revolt was crushed. Spartacus was killed, and more than 6,000 rebel slaves were crucified along the road from Capua to Rome.

This brutal retaliation was intended to discourage slaves from the thought of resistance, but it had the opposite effect. Roman slaves fought more fiercely than ever for their liberty, with the efforts of Spartacus serving as an inspiration. The efforts failed, but for nearly 2,000 years the heroic and tragic story of Spartacus has remained a beacon of hope to the oppressed.

But practical reasons were not the only ones used to defend slavery in America. Intellectuals looked to ancient philosophy and found support in the writings of Plato and Aristotle, both of whom believed some were born to rule, others to serve. In the fourth century B.C., Aristotle wrote in his book *Politics* that "The lower sort are by nature slaves, and it is better for them . . . that they should be under the rule of a master."

Greek philosophers approved of slavery, but only for non-Greeks; similarly, white Americans thought it right to enslave others only if they were of "lesser" races. Scientific thought before the 20th century was almost unanimous in believing that Africans were naturally inferior and therefore incapable of taking an equal place in society. Carolus Linnaeus, the 18th-century founder of the modern system of scientific classification of plants and animals, classified African pygmies along with mandrills among the "tailless apes."

Some proponents made a moral case for slavery by quoting scripture. Christian churchmen pointed out that in Leviticus 25:44–46 God commands, "of the heathen . . . shall ye buy bondmen and bondmaids. . . . And ye shall take them as an inheritance for your children after you, to inherit them as a possession." Boston theologian John Saffin wrote in 1777 that the abolition of slavery in America would "invert the order that God hath set in the world, who hath ordained different degrees and orders of men."◆

## Slavery in Medieval Times

In the Middle Ages, as the Roman Empire disintegrated and modern nations emerged, slavery in Europe changed form. Agricultural workers in France, Spain, Italy, Germany, and Russia became serfs, owing both service and taxes in return for the right to work the soil. Although they could not be sold off their land, they did not own it, and they were bound to their lords almost as completely as ancient slaves had belonged to their masters. This form of slavery continued in Russia until 1861.

In Asia and the Near East, slavery was a long-established institution, and the wars between East and West increased the numbers of slaves. The Crusades, clashes between European Christians and Near Eastern Muslims from the 11th to the 13th centuries, brought slavery to new heights. Both sides captured and sold soldiers and civilians.

During the 16th century, the Ottoman Empire was the most powerful in the world. Based in present-day Turkey, it stretched from Iran across North Africa to central Europe. Ruled by the Sultan, who held all the agricultural land as his personal property, the empire's government had slavery at its foundation. The Ottoman Turks, who were Muslims, imposed an annual tax of 1,000 to 3,000 male children on all Christian populations in the Balkans. These slaves were trained, with others conquered in war, not only to fight but to conduct business and govern. The best fighters among these slaves became the sultan's personal guard, while the most skillful administrators held the top offices in the government.

## Slavery in Africa

Like the nations of Europe and Asia, the many kingdoms and empires of Africa had employed slavery since ancient times. Convicted criminals and captives taken in tribal wars were forced into bondage and sold. Arabs, working in partnership with African rulers, had conducted a trade in human beings since before the beginning of the Christian era. As the market grew, people were kidnapped and tribal wars were fought for slaves, a more valuable property than livestock or land.

African slaves were first brought to Christian Europe in 1444, when Prince Henry of Portugal accepted a boatload of Africans in exchange for some Arab prisoners. From that date on, slaves were regularly imported from Africa into Spain and Portugal to work on farms. Portuguese explorers brought as many as a thousand black slaves a year to the

European market in the last half of the 15th century. By 1550, Africans accounted for more than half the population of Lisbon, the Portuguese capital.

## Slavery in the New World

In 1492, when Columbus first set sail for the New World, the African slave trade in Europe was already well established—so much so that one of Columbus's objectives was to find new sources of slaves for the king of Spain.

With the discovery of the Americas, many things changed in Europe. There were vast new prospects for adventure and fortune in the New World; rich lands were available to anyone who could tame them and make them pay. But to profit from the newfound riches of the Americas it was necessary to develop the land. In the 1490s, the Spanish established the first colonies in the New World, settling in

*The first slaves in the New World were captive Native Americans.* (New York Public Library Picture Collection)

Hispaniola, the island now occupied by Haiti and the Dominican Republic. The soil was good and there were mineral resources, but the Spanish had not come to work as farmers or miners themselves; they enslaved the native population to do the actual work of panning for gold and tilling the soil.

For several reasons it was not a very successful venture. First, some native tribes were warriors and fought fiercely against enslavement. Others were more easily subdued but still did not take well to forced labor. They were not used to the kind of work the Spaniards demanded, or to the diseases they brought with them. Many rebelled under the Spanish lash and refused to obey orders. Others became sick and died. And because the slaves were in their own country, they knew the land better than their conquerors and were able to escape back to their villages. Even with the superior weapons of Europe, the Spaniards could not make the natives work very effectively.

In 1515, a Spanish missionary named Bartolomé de Las Casas wrote to Emperor Charles V from Hispaniola urging him to abolish Indian slavery. It was not only humane motives that prompted the priest's suggestion but also the observation that enslaving Indians just wasn't profitable. Instead, he proposed that the emperor send Africans to work in the colony. A few Africans had already been sent to the New World and forced into slavery to replace the Indians who had escaped or been killed. The emperor agreed to the proposal, and the African slave trade with the Americas began. Licenses were issued to Spanish noblemen to import slaves from Africa to the colonies of the New World.

Slavery was too profitable a business to remain without competition for long, and soon other nations began participating. A stream of slaves began to pour into Hispaniola, the West Indies and North and South America, imported by the English, the French, and the Dutch as well as by the Spanish and Portuguese. It is estimated that by 1600 over 44,000 African slaves were being imported annually to Brazil alone.

The first census of Brazil, taken in 1798, counted over 2 million blacks in a total population of 3.25 million.

## Slavery in English North America

Before the English came, there were Spanish settlements in North America that were built and maintained with the aid of African slaves. Slavery would come later to the English colonies. The first English settlement in North America was Jamestown, founded in 1607 in the present-day state of Virginia. Jamestown had no slaves, but there were white servants in the colony who had come from England with contracts, called indentures, to work for set periods of time before they were wholly "free."

The first Africans to appear in English North America arrived in Jamestown aboard a Dutch ship in 1619. There were about 20 of them, and they were sold as indentured servants to work on the plantations of the colony under contracts similar to those of the English servants. In five to seven years they could satisfy the terms of their indentures and become free settlers. Some became independent farmers, working their own land; others earned livings as craftsmen, merchants, or trappers. All had the same rights as their white neighbors.

The form slavery took for these first African Americans did not last long in North America. As the number and size of tobacco and sugar plantations grew in the English colonies, the need for labor grew too. The English colonists wanted permanent workers who would not require wages. European diseases had greatly thinned the ranks of Native Americans, whom the colonists found it easier to push westward than to enslave. Soon a thriving slave trade developed between Africa and the Americas.

Triangle Trade Route, Late 1700s

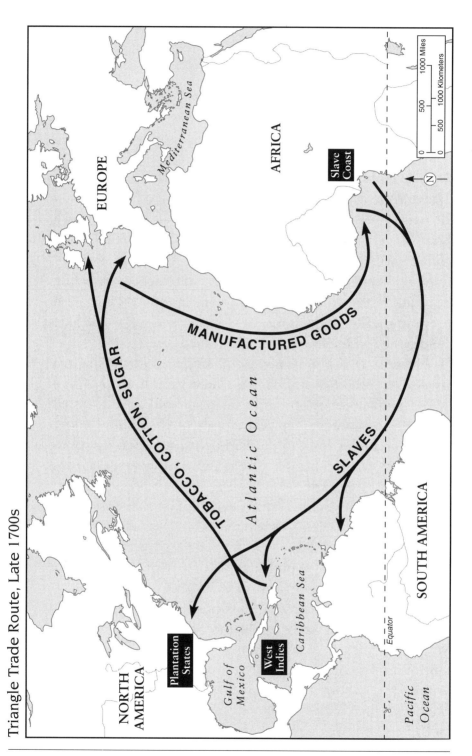

## The Triangle Trade

By the beginning of the 18th century, transporting slaves from Africa to the Americas had become the most profitable maritime activity. The English developed a regular route that was known as the triangle trade because it had three stages. A ship left its home port in England or continental Europe with a cargo of manufactured goods—usually guns, liquor, cloth, and tools—and sailed to West Africa. There the merchandise was traded for slaves. Then came the second stage, called the Middle Passage, across the Atlantic to either the West Indies or the colonies in North America. There the human cargo, or whatever part of it had survived the dreadful voyage, was sold. The ship was then loaded with sugar, rice, or tobacco for the voyage home to Europe that completed the triangle.

Conditions during the Middle Passage were so bad that a large percentage of slaves—some place the figure at more than half—died on the way. If there was a good supply of human merchandise on the African coast, the slaves were treated like livestock, squeezed between decks or stored on improvised shelves, and often kept in chains throughout the voyage. Many slaves took their own lives rather than submit. One British statesman and opponent of slavery, Sir William Wilberforce, was so horrified by the conditions he discovered that he appealed to the conscience of the House of Commons in 1789:

> The transit of the slaves to the West Indies . . . is the most wretched part of the whole subject. Let anyone imagine to himself six or seven hundred of these wretches chained two and two, surrounded with every object that is nauseous and disgusting, . . . diseased and struggling under every kind of wretchedness! Death, at least, is a sure ground of evidence, and the proportion

of deaths will not only confirm, but if possible will even aggravate our suspicion of their misery in transit.

A dramatic example of the brutality of the Middle Passage is the case of the *Zong*, a ship carrying 400 slaves from the African coast to the island of Jamaica in 1781. The trip was a long and difficult one, and many became ill on the way. Seven whites and more than 60 Africans died during the first two and a half months of the passage. The captain, Luke Collingwood, realized that the ship was running out of fresh water. He knew the ship's insurance policy covered loss of cargo from drowning but not from thirst, so the insurance company would pay for any slaves thrown overboard to save drinking water. Accordingly he selected the weakest, had their hands tied behind them, and ordered them cast into the sea. In all he disposed of 122 slaves in this manner. Ten more took their own lives as the crew prepared them to be thrown over the side. The insurance company had to pay the ship owners £30 for each slave "lost."

## Beginnings of Slave Rebellion in the New World

Resistance was almost impossible during the Middle Passage, yet the nearly helpless passengers on those voyages often rebelled. Some tried to jump overboard and swim to shore, others refused to eat; many attacked their guards even though they knew there was little chance of success. One modern history reports over 150 rebellions on board slave ships, though it was not until the 19th century that any of them succeeded.

Rebellion—on sea and on land—goes back to the very beginnings of American slavery. The first slave insurrection in the present boundaries of the United States took place in the first American colony that included African slaves. In 1526 the Spanish explorer Lucas Vásquez de Ayllón left

Hispaniola to establish a colony in what is now South Carolina. He brought with him 500 Spaniards and 100 African slaves. The natives of the area, angered at the seizure of their lands, made frequent raids on the Spanish and encouraged the Africans to join them. Illness further weakened the settlers. Many died, including their leader, Ayllón. After a few months, the slaves organized a rebellion, killed some of the Spanish, and escaped to live among the Indians. Their departure was more than the colony could endure. Only 150 of the Spaniards survived, and, without slaves to work for them, the survivors gave up the settlement and returned to Hispaniola.

Resistance, in small ways and large, was common among African slaves in all the New World colonies. Many small uprisings are recorded in the early days of the English colonies in America, despite Africans' being badly outnumbered until near the end of the 17th century. In 1663, for example, the Virginia colony held only about 1,000 Africans—less than 5 percent of the population. Yet a large-scale rebellion was planned in Virginia for September of that year. The uprising never took place, but not from lack of determination on the part of the rebels. The plan fell apart when a slave named John Berkenhead told his master about the conspiracy. This type of informing became typical, thwarting many slave rebellions.

The Virginia colonists had lived in fear of rebellion and so were prepared to act quickly in response to the attempted uprising. The authorities rounded up and hanged the ringleaders without a trial. Then they

> *W*e stood in arms, firing on the revolted slaves of whom we killed some, and wounded many: which so terrified the rest that they gave way . . . ; and many of the most mutinous leapt overboard, and drowned themselves in the ocean with much resolution, showing no manner of concern for life.
>
>
>
> John Barbot, captain of the English slave ship *Don Carlos*, describing a slave mutiny, 1701

*The deck of the slave ship* Wildfire, *intercepted in American waters in 1860 carrying 560 African slaves. From a daguerreotype in* Harper's Weekly, *June 2, 1860.* (Library of Congress)

gave John Berkenhead his freedom and 5,000 pounds of tobacco as a reward for betraying the conspiracy. By offering such a generous reward, the colonists hoped to encourage other Africans to report any planned revolts. The government of the colony passed a law declaring the day John Berkenhead reported the conspiracy a holiday, celebrating "the preserving of all we have from utter ruin." The law read, "Resolved, that the 13th of September be annually kept holy, being the day those villains intended to put the plot into execution."

Reports exist of similar uprisings, or planned uprisings, in 1687 and 1710, and undoubtedly others occurred that have left no records. None of these plots succeeded, but they made the white settlers nervous. The colonists knew they were living on shaky ground. After the 1687 conspiracy was uncovered, the Virginia House of Burgesses passed a law banning public funerals for slaves. The aim was to prevent large gatherings of Africans. Every bid for freedom by the slave populace was met with still harsher repression, but the resistance never ceased. These small rebellions did nothing to improve slave conditions or to discourage white settlers from keeping slaves, but they kept the spirit of independence and the quest for freedom alive.

## NOTES

p. 11  "The transit of the slaves . . ." Speech by Sir William Wilberforce to the House of Commons, London, May 12, 1799, quoted in Houston Peterson, ed., *A Treasury of the World's Great Speeches* (New York: Simon & Schuster, 1954), p. 213.

p. 15  "Resolved, that the 13th of September . . ." *Journal of the Virginia House of Burgesses 1659–1693*, quoted in Joseph Cephas Carroll, *Slave Insurrections in the United States* (1938; New York: Negro Universities Press, 1968), p. 14.

2

# What They Resisted: Slave Life in America

The first laborers in the American colonies were the colonists themselves. During most of the 17th century they depended on their own efforts or hired workers from Europe. All the colonies tried imposing forced labor on Native Americans but never made satisfactory slaves of them. The 20 Africans whose indentures were sold to the Jamestown colony in 1619 were not slaves, but had been contracted to work for limited periods of time. Few Africans followed them to North America during the next half century.

In those days the Portuguese and Dutch dominated the slave trade. Their merchandise was too expensive for most English settlers. But as the sources of contract workers began to dry up in Europe and the need for labor in North America grew, the market for African workers in the English colonies increased. By the end of the 17th century the English had increased their share of the profitable slave trade, and African slaves soon replaced Europeans in the work force of the English colonies. In 1680, some 4 percent of the population of the American colonies was African; by 1770, Africans and African Americans made up almost 20 percent of the total non-Indian population of North America. In South Carolina they accounted for more than 60 percent. By the time of the Revolutionary War, the black populations of Georgia, Virginia, the Carolinas, and Maryland were as large as or larger than the white populations.

## Slavery in the Colonies

Before the Revolutionary War, African slaves existed in all American colonies and were essential to the economy. The majority were in the South, where an agricultural economy depended on their labor as field hands. In the North, African slaves were more likely to be found in the cities, working as household servants or craftsmen.

At first there were no laws governing the rights and responsibilities of slaves and owners, but in time formal slave codes emerged. These codes differed from place to place, as each colony established its own rules. But two basic principles made slavery in the New World uniform while making it distinct from the slavery common in ancient and medieval times or in Africa. In the American colonies, in both the North and the South, slavery was based on race—it was legal to enslave Indians and Africans, but not white people; and it was hereditary—the child of a slave was born a slave.

## Slavery in the South

Such colonies as Virginia and South Carolina, where large numbers of Africans were concentrated, developed stricter laws than the Northern colonies. Slaves in the South were forbidden to possess firearms, to travel the roads without written passes from their white owners, or to gather together in groups without white supervision. In these colonies, Africans had no protection in the courts.

## Slavery in the North

In the colonies north of Maryland, the legal codes governing slavery were much less restrictive. The people of New England respected the principle of equal justice and wrote it into their laws. African slaves could own private property and they could will it to friends and relatives. In some states, slaves were allowed to testify against whites in court and were entitled to legal counsel and a trial by jury if charged with a crime. While Southern slave owners were free to punish slaves in any way they chose and were almost never prosecuted for causing their death, New York passed a law in 1686 making the deliberate killing of a slave a capital crime. In Maine in 1694, a white master was charged with murder for causing the death of his slave through "Cruell Beating and hard usage." He was convicted of manslaughter and

The treatment of slaves was different at the North from the South; at the North they were admitted to be a species of the human family.

James Mars, *Life of James Mars, a Slave Born and Sold in Connecticut* (1869)

*Slaves had no legal protection from the brutality of their owners.* (Library of Congress)

fined 10 pounds and 10 shillings—not a very severe punishment, but evidence that the courts recognized the slave as a human being.

## Slavery after the Revolutionary War

As the colonists began to agitate for freedom from England, a few patriots recognized the moral case against slavery in America. People began to notice the contradiction between demanding independence for themselves and holding others as slaves. Among the many pamphlets attacking British tyranny, there were some that called attention to the embarrassing parallel between English treatment of Americans and American treatment of Africans. The Baptist minister John Allen wrote in 1774,

> Blush, ye pretended votaries for freedom! ye trifling patriots! who are making a vain parade of being advocates for the liberties of mankind, who are thus making a mockery of your profession by trampling on the sacred rights and privileges of Africans; for while you are

fasting, praying . . . , and pleading for a restoration of your charter rights, you are at the same time continuing this lawless, cruel, inhuman, and abominable practice of enslaving your fellow creatures.

Benjamin Franklin formed an antislavery organization in Pennsylvania, and both George Washington and Thomas Jefferson publicly expressed philosophical dislike for slavery, though they did not free the slaves they themselves owned. In Massachusetts the colonial legislature voted twice to end the slave trade, first in 1771 and later in 1774, but each time the governor of the colony vetoed the decision. Rhode Island declared its slaves free, Delaware prohibited the importation of new slaves, and Pennsylvania imposed such high taxes on the importation of slaves that the trade was effectively ended there. In April 1776, the Continental Congress voted to end the importation of slaves throughout the 13 colonies.

After the Revolutionary War, one by one the Northern states passed laws abolishing slavery. South of the Mason-Dixon Line—the line running between Pennsylvania and Maryland that divides North and South—no such laws were passed. The legislatures of Maryland and Virginia did vote on proposals to end slavery, but in both states these were defeated. By 1804 the country had become clearly divided: Slavery was illegal in the nine Northern states but still flourished in the eight Southern ones. A few plantation owners in the South opposed the institution on moral grounds and privately freed their own slaves, but the region's agrarian economy still depended very heavily on slave labor.

## Free African Americans

Even "free" African Americans were not completely free. In 1790 there were nearly 60,000 non-slave Africans and African Americans in the young nation, living in both the North and the South. Some had been born free, the descendants of freed slaves. Others had been granted their freedom for having served in the Revolutionary War, or had been released by their owners. A few had bought their freedom with money earned from private work. But, though legally free, these people were generally not much better off than their enslaved brethren.

The legal status of free African Americans differed from state to state. Their condition was worse in the South, where the tradition of white mastery still reigned and where they were feared as a possible source of agitation among slaves. Free African Americans were required to carry documented proof of their freedom wherever they went in the South, and sometimes had to have "FREE" branded on their shoulders. They were not permitted to hold public office, vote, testify in court against whites (except in Delaware and Louisiana), or own firearms. In some areas they could not buy or drink alcohol. Everywhere they were forbidden to be out at night without a written pass, or to assemble except in their own churches.

*Free African Americans were often kidnapped and sold into slavery in both the North and the South.* (Library of Congress)

In the North, life for free African Americans was somewhat easier, but was still restricted. Only in Maine, Massachusetts, New Hampshire, and Vermont could African Americans vote (in New York, voting was limited to those who owned at least $250 worth of real estate). In five states they could not testify against whites in court. African Americans had to post a $500 bond to cross the border into Ohio, and a $1,000 bond to set foot in Illinois; they could not enter Indiana or Oregon at all. Everywhere, in the North and the South, the public schools were closed to their children, and they were limited to the lowest-paying jobs, when they could find even those.

One of the special problems for free African Americans was that their color made them subject to being kidnapped and sold into slavery. There were strict laws against this practice, even in the South—in North Carolina a white man was hanged for selling a freed slave in 1806—but it was difficult to prevent or to prove. When the legal slave trade was abolished and the supply of labor dwindled, the price of slaves went up. One scholar estimates that an unskilled male sold for about $600 in 1820 and for $1,500 some 30 years later.

The U.S. Constitution nowhere uses the word slavery, but it recognizes the institution and permits it indirectly. Section 2 of Article IV authorizes slave owners to recapture runaways, even in states where slavery is illegal. It was easy to seize a black man, destroy his identification papers, and claim him as a slave. Because it was almost impossible for African Americans to bring charges against whites in court, the kidnapper's claim was almost impossible to disprove.

No person held to service or labor in one State, under the laws thereof, escaping into another, shall, in consequence of any law or regulation therein, be discharged from any service or labor, but shall be delivered up on claim of the party to whom such service or labor may be due.

◆

U.S. Constitution, Article IV,
Section 2, Paragraph 3

A famous case was that of Solomon Northrup, a second-generation free black man born in New York. Northrup was drugged and sold to a slave dealer in 1841. When he awoke in chains and demanded his freedom, the dealer stripped him, forced him face down onto a bench, and beat him with a hardwood board. "Blow after blow he inflicted on my naked body," Northrup recalled many years later. "When his unrelenting arm grew tired, he stopped and asked if I still insisted I was a free man. I did insist upon it, and then the blows were renewed." Northrup had no legal way to prove that he was a free man, and he spent 12 years as a slave before friends from the North restored him to freedom and to his family.

## Slave Life

Although many former slaves like Northrup, as well as slave owners and visitors to the South, wrote their recollections after the Civil War, the conditions of life on Southern plantations remain a subject of historical controversy. One reason for this is that different people presented very different pictures.

Southern whites naturally tried to prove that slaves were well treated and even happy. Novels and songs portrayed slave owners as behaving like loving fathers to their slaves, and depicted slaves as carefree and devoted to their masters. Scholars pointed to the slaves' love of song to prove how much they enjoyed their lives and how much mutual affection there was between them and their owners. George Fitzhugh, a Virginia slave owner and sociologist, wrote in 1850, "There is no . . . war between master and slave. The slaves are all well fed, well clad, have plenty of fuel, and are happy. They have no dread of the future—no fear of want. . . . The relation of master and slave is one of mutual good will."

But the evidence does not generally support this picture. Although there were kind and loving slaveholders, and some

# American Slavery As It Is _____

We know a great deal about American slavery, from many different sources. Some slaves wrote their recollections after they escaped or were freed. Visitors from other countries reported what they saw in their travels. Opponents of slavery produced a huge body of literature emphasizing its horrors, and slave owners wrote pamphlets in an attempt to make a case for the system. Most accounts are strongly biased, so historians have had to analyze all these documents carefully to try to get an accurate picture of how American slavery worked.

The fullest examination of slavery written in the 19th century, and the most reliable, was Theodore Weld's *American Slavery As It Is: Testimony of a Thousand Witnesses*, published in New York by the Anti-Slavery Society in 1839. Described as "the most crushing indictment of any institution ever written," it was remarkable for its careful documentation and its scrupulous honesty.

Weld was opposed to slavery, but he was determined to produce a fair account of it. As he said in his introduction, "We shall establish

of their human property were content, the lives of slaves were seldom the pleasant ones depicted in Southern propaganda. More than 90 percent of slaves in 19th-century America worked on plantations under the strictest and most painful conditions. Household servants might share some of their owner's comforts, but most slaves were field hands, forced to work from dawn to sunset under the whip of an overseer. Poorly fed, minimally dressed, and lodged in the meanest shacks, they were treated no better than farm animals. In 1845, former slave Frederick Douglass described in very exact terms the living conditions on the rich Maryland plantation where he spent his childhood:

> The men and women slaves received, as their monthly allowance of food, eight pounds of pork, or its equiva-

these facts by the testimony of scores and hundreds of eye witnesses, by the testimony of *slaveholders* in all parts of the slave states, by slaveholding members of Congress and of state legislatures, by judges, by doctors of divinity, . . . by merchants, mechanics, lawyers and physicians." He wrote to people everywhere for evidence, and checked all answers carefully, providing names and dates for every detail. He also scrutinized court records and the complete files of dozens of Southern newspapers.

The results proved, as Weld states, "that the slaves in the United States are treated with barbarous inhumanity, that they are overworked, underfed, wretchedly clad and lodged . . . that they are often kept confined in stocks day and night, have some of their front teeth knocked out or broken off that they may be easily detected when they run away; that they are frequently flogged with terrible severity." Weld proved beyond question that the picture Southerners presented of well-treated, contented slaves was a cruel lie.

The publication of *American Slavery As It Is* caused a sensation. It sold more than 100,000 copies during its first year and became the handbook for antislavery crusaders.◆

lent in fish, and one bushel of corn meal. Their yearly clothing consisted of two coarse linen shirts, one pair of linen trousers, . . . one pair of trousers for winter, . . . one pair of stockings, and one pair of shoes; the whole of which could not have cost more than seven dollars. . . . The children unable to work in the field had neither shoes, stockings, jackets, nor trousers, given to them; their clothing consisted of two course linen shirts per year. When these failed them, they went naked. . . . There were no beds given the slaves.

But such discomforts were far from the worst that slaves had to endure. Douglass, like many other writers about life on Southern plantations, described scenes of savage cruelty by his owners. Of one owner he recalled, "He would at times seem to take great pleasure in whipping a slave. I have often

*Separation of families was one of the most tragic aspects of slavery.* (New York Public Library Picture Collection)

been awakened at the dawn of the day by the most heart-rending shrieks of an own aunt of mine, whom he used to tie up to a joist, and whip upon her naked back till she was literally covered with blood. . . . He would whip her to make her scream, and whip her to make her hush; and not until overcome by fatigue, would he cease to swing the blood-clotted cowskin."

Psychological pain could be as bitter as physical pain. Slave owners recognized the danger to their authority posed by family loyalty among slaves, and they did their best to prevent the emotional support it provided. Slaves were encouraged to have children, who brought a profit to an owner by increasing his holdings, and young men and women were sometimes locked up together at night, like livestock, to breed. But marriage between slaves was not recognized and had no legal protection. It was almost impossible for slaves to establish stable families.

White masters had the power to rape slave women. There was little either the woman or her mate could do about it without risking severe punishment and even death. As Henry Bibb, a slave who escaped to the North, wrote in 1850, "A poor slave's wife can never be . . . true to her husband contrary to the will of her master. . . . She dare not refuse to be reduced to a state of adultry." Slave owners could also break up slave families by selling their members separately. According to records of slave marriages in Mississippi, Tennessee, and Louisiana in the 1860s, nearly one third were dissolved by slave owners, most within their first five years. Slave owners separated husbands from wives and often sold mothers away from their children. A child's tears or a mother's pleas had little effect in such cases. The experience of Frederick Douglass was typical: Separated from his mother when he was an infant—"a common custom," he reported—he saw her only four or five times afterward, when she sneaked by night to where he lived—walking 12 miles without shoes—to spend a few minutes with him. "I do not recollect of ever seeing my mother by the light of day," he recalled.

Owners were afraid of slaves' forming strong family bonds, but they were even more afraid of social organization among their workers. In most areas, slaves were not permitted to assemble, even for church services or funerals. This was to prevent them from plotting. To prevent escapes, the Southern states passed laws prohibiting slaves from all free movement. If Frederick Douglass's

I have often been utterly astonished, since I came to the North, to find persons who could speak of the singing, among slaves, as evidence of their contentment and happiness. It is impossible to conceive of a greater mistake. . . . The songs of the slave represent the sorrows of his heart; and he is relieved by them, only as an aching heart is relieved by its tears.

Frederick Douglass, *Narrative of the Life of Frederick Douglass, an American Slave* (1845)

mother had been caught visiting him, she would have been beaten. Slaves were kept at work during the day and isolated in their quarters at night. A system of patrols was established to maintain this isolation.

Slave owners also feared that slaves might learn to read and write. Owners feared that if slaves could read they might come across pamphlets attacking slavery and might get dangerous ideas about their own right to freedom. Most Southern states had laws against teaching slaves; one passed in South Carolina in 1740 made such instruction a crime punishable by a £100 fine. The official reason for this was that a literate slave could write himself a pass to buy liquor, or to sell his services privately as a craftsman, or to be out of quarters at night and so escape. But most of all, slave owners feared that slaves who could communicate by letter might plot rebellion.

Frederick Douglass was one of the few slaves who learned to read and write, and his recollections of the process gives us a clear idea of Southern thinking at the time. A kind mistress, he wrote, "commenced to teach me the A, B, C," but when her husband found out about it he told her to stop, because it was not only illegal but unsafe to teach a slave to read. As the slave owner explained,

> A nigger should know nothing but to obey his master—to do as he is told to do. Learning would *spoil* the best nigger in the world. Now . . . if you teach that nigger . . . how to read, there would be no keeping him. It would forever unfit him to be a slave. He would at once become unmanageable, and of no value to his

master. And to himself, it would do him no good, but a great deal of harm. It would make him discontented and unhappy.

Douglass's owner was right—learning to read did spoil slaves and make them unmanageable. But he was wrong about education making slaves unhappy. Those who managed to learn despite the overwhelming obstacles found that education helped them realize and sustain a belief in their rights as human beings. It also strengthened the conviction that there might be something they could do to attain these rights.

## NOTES

p. 19 "Blush, ye pretended votaries for freedom . . ." John Allen, *The Watchman's Alarm to Lord N—-th* (1774), quoted in Bernard Bailyn, *The Origins of the American Revolution* (Cambridge, Mass.: Harvard University Press, 1967), p. 240.

p. 23 "Blow after blow he inflicted . . ." Solomon Northrup, *Twelve Years a Slave* (1853; Baton Rouge, La.: Louisiana State University Press, 1968), p. 23.

p. 23 "There is no . . . war . . ." George Fitzhugh, *Sociology of the South, or The Failure of Free Society* (1854), quoted in Eric L. McKitrick, ed., *Slavery Defended: The Views of the Old South* (Englewood Cliffs, N.J.: Prentice-Hall, 1963), p. 45.

p. 24–25 "The men and women slaves . . ." Frederick Douglass, *Narrative of the Life of Frederick Douglass, an American Slave* (1845; Garden City, N.Y.: Doubleday, 1963), p. 10.

p. 25–26 "He would at times seem to take great pleasure . . ." Douglass, p. 5.

p. 27 "A poor slave's wife . . ." Henry Bibb, Narrative of the *Life and Adventures of Henry Bibb, an American Slave* (1850; Salem, N.H.; Ayer, 1991), pp. 191–92.

p. 28–29 "A nigger should know nothing . . ." Douglass, p. 36.

# 3

# *How They Resisted: Fighting the System*

$T$he pretty picture Southern-
ers painted of contented slaves loyally serving their beloved
masters was convincing to many in the North. One argument
used to support this view was the claim that there were few
organized rebellions against slavery. But the evidence on the
other side—the evidence that most slaves were profoundly
unhappy with their situation and did everything they could
to resist—is much stronger.

It is true that reports of large-scale slave revolts were rare.
This is not surprising, considering how difficult it was for
slaves to organize rebellion, and how careful slave owners
were to keep any evidence of rebellion from being reported.

*Supporters of slavery presented a romantic picture of slave conditions.*   (Library of Congress)

But armed insurrection was merely one form of resistance. There is ample evidence that slaves fought back in many less dramatic ways.

Probably the easiest and safest way slaves resisted was simply by working slowly and being deliberately careless. This form of resistance was one of the most frustrating to slave owners. It didn't bother slaves to be considered lazy or stupid; they had the last laugh as they dragged out simple jobs for hours. Slaves more than demonstrated their energy and intelligence when they had the chance to work for themselves. Frederick Douglass made it clear that slaves consciously rebelled in this way, writing, "As the master studies to keep the slave ignorant, the slave is cunning enough to make the master think he succeeds."

Another simple and unprovable way for slaves to fight their owners was by pretending sickness. The records of Southern planters are full of irritated notes like that of

George Washington, who in a letter to his steward written while he was president complained that his female slaves would "lay up a month, at the end of which no visible change in their countenance, nor the loss of an ounce of flesh, is discoverable; and their allowance of provision is going on as if nothing ailed them." Occasionally these ways of avoiding work were carried to more drastic extremes. Slaves desperate to avoid certain jobs sometimes deliberately injured themselves, breaking limbs or cutting off fingers to make work impossible.

The ultimate act of desperate defiance was suicide. Southern records contain many accounts of slaves driven to this terrible end when they lost all hope of freedom. One worker on a Georgia rice plantation threw himself into a river and drowned himself rather than undergo another whipping. The overseer ordered that the body be left where it was to show the others what happened to such disobedient slaves. The records of the Virginia House of Burgesses include no fewer than 55 claims submitted between 1700 and 1800 by slave owners asking to be reimbursed for the value of slaves who had killed themselves. Suicide was especially frequent among newly arrived slaves. The decision to commit suicide rather than endure slavery was in some instances a collective act. Several cases of mass suicide are recorded during the 18th and 19th centuries. In 1807, two boatloads of Africans in Charleston, South Carolina starved themselves to death.

## Sabotage

While slaves sometimes resorted to self-destructive behavior, they more frequently engaged in behavior that was destructive to their owners. Probably the most common form of slave resistance was what historians have labeled "silent sabotage"—small, secret acts of defiance that slave owners could not prove and sometimes could not even recognize.

Windows and agricultural implements broke mysteriously, food and household items disappeared, gates were left open allowing livestock to escape, crops burned, boats drifted away. Many planters stopped using plows on their farms because something always seemed to go wrong with them. Life on Southern plantations was often a continuous battle of wits between slaves and their owners.

Open, large-scale sabotage was less common, but it was a serious problem for plantation owners. Because slaves usually prepared and served the household's food, they had ready opportunities for poisoning an especially cruel master. They also had the expertise. Many slaves had brought with them from Africa extensive knowledge of dangerous plants that could be used for this purpose.

Even more alarming to owners was the threat of arson, considered one of the greatest dangers in the South before the Civil War. While it was almost impossible for slaves to get guns or other weapons, anyone could start a fire. Houses and barns—especially those of unpopular owners—burned down with suspicious frequency. So great was the danger that the American Fire Insurance Company of Philadelphia refused even to write policies in the slave states.

## Confrontations

Although numerous slaves were convicted of arson in the South during the 18th and 19th centuries, we can never be sure how many fires were deliberately set as acts of protest or vengeance and how many were accidents or the result of slave indifference and negligence. More clear-cut proof of slaves' dissatisfaction were the open confrontations that occurred when slaves were pushed too far. These were not planned rebellions, motivated by the hope of freedom, but rather explosions of anger. There are few reports of direct defiance by slaves in the records of their owners, for obvious reasons: Such challenges to white authority were an embarrassment; in addition, public knowledge of these confrontations could prompt other slaves to take similar actions. But reports of visitors to the South and the memoirs of former slaves contain many accounts of workers who stood up to their owners and fought.

An African named George provides an early example of a slave who simply refused to submit. The agent trying to sell him at a slave market in Reading, Pennsylvania in 1772 wrote his owner that George "protested publickly that he would not be sold, and if Any one should purchase him he wou'd be the death of him and words to like purpose which deter'd the people from bidding." Because of his defiance, George was kept in jail, "almost Naked . . . Chain'd & Hand cuff'd on Account of his Threats." We do not know what happened to him.

Open insubordination usually met with drastic retaliation, but it nevertheless occurred more often than Southern slave owners were willing to admit. The kidnapped slave Solomon Northrup reported several cases in which, "goaded into uncontrollable madness, even the slave will sometimes turn upon his oppressor." One example was a lad who, through no fault of his own, took longer with a job than his overseer thought proper and was ordered to strip for a flogging. "The boy submitted," Northrup wrote, "until maddened at such injustice, and insane with pain, he sprang to his feet, and seizing an axe, literally chopped the overseer in pieces." Then he calmly reported the act to his owner and, when led to the gallows to be hung, "maintained an undismayed and fearless bearing, and with his last words justified the act."

When whites administered severe punishment to defiant slaves, they were acting not just from anger, but also with a determination to prevent such rebelliousness from becoming an example to others. Frederick Douglass reported a horrendous incident from his own slave days. His overseer, a cruel man appropriately named Gore, was a natural slave driver who, according to Douglass, "was just the man for such a place, and it was just the place for such a man." One day Gore ordered one lashing too many for a slave named Demby. Unable to endure another whipping, Demby ran into a creek and refused to come out. Gore gave him three calls and then "without consultation or deliberation with anyone . . . raised his musket to his face, taking deadly aim at his standing victim, and in an instant poor Demby was no more. His mangled body sank out of sight, and blood and brains marked the water where he had stood." Gore was not reprimanded by his employer, the owner of the slave. The overseer explained to the owner, Douglass relates, that Demby "was setting a dangerous example to the other slaves, one which . . . would finally lead to the total subversion of all rule and order upon the plantation. He [the overseer] argued that if one slave refused to be corrected, and escaped with his life, the other slaves would soon copy the example."

The consequences of direct confrontation with authority were not always so brutal. Sometimes such a clash had the happy result of not only preserving a slave's spirit of independence but actually winning him some relief. When James Mars, at the age of 16, was threatened with a whipping he felt to be unjustified, he merely told his master, "You had better not!" and walked out the door. Apparently the mere suggestion of resistance was enough. "From that time until I was twenty-one," he reported in his autobiogra-

The amount of work expected of a field hand will not be more than one half of what would be demanded of a white man; and even that will not be properly done unless he be constantly overlooked.

T. D. Ozanne, *The South As It Is* (1863)

phy, "I do not remember that he ever gave me an unpleasant word or look."

Frederick Douglass's memoirs give an example that illustrates an important fact about the psychology of both the slave and the master. The youthful Douglass had been hired out to a planter known as a cruel "negro-breaker" and had patiently endured six months of abuse. At last his tolerance reached its limit. Faced with one more undeserved whipping, he turned on his master. "At that moment," he wrote, "—from whence came the spirit I don't know—I resolved to fight." Slave and master fought furiously for two hours, Douglass getting very much the better of it. "He asked me if I meant to persist in my resistance," Douglass recalled. "I told him I did, come what might; that he had used me like a brute for six months, and that I was determined to be used so no longer." Seeing that he had lost not only the fight but the psychological advantage of master over slave, the planter gave up. "This battle," wrote Douglass,

> was the turning point in my career as a slave. It rekindled the few expiring embers of freedom, and revived within me a sense of my own manhood. . . . The gratification afforded by the triumph was a full compensation for whatever else might follow, even death itself. He can only understand the deep satisfaction which I experienced, who has himself repelled by force the bloody arm of slavery. . . . I now resolved that, however long I might remain a slave in form, the day had passed forever when I could be a slave in fact. . . . The white man who expected to succeed in whipping, must also succeed in killing me.

Douglass remained with the negro-breaker for six months more, but never felt the touch of his lash again. In fact, he reported, "From this time I was never again what might be called fairly whipped, though I remained a slave four years

afterward. I had several fights, but I was never whipped."
From this experience he learned a valuable lesson, that even
if defying oppression did not win a slave respect or sympathy,
it earned him a degree of self-respect and safety. Slave owners
and overseers were afraid of the embarrassment of defeat.
This sometimes meant they did not want to take the risk of
tangling with a slave who stood up for himself. "He is
whipped oftenest," Douglass concluded, "who is whipped
easiest."

## Escape

Escape often proved a more rewarding way of asserting
independence than attacking a master. There was rarely any
support for the slave who confronted his master with physi-

Ann Wood *fought off a posse of slave-hunters while escaping to the North from*
Loudon County, Virginia, Christmas Eve, 1855.   (Library of Congress)

cal violence; even sympathetic whites remained unwilling to go against their own people by helping a slave in a fight, and fellow slaves were usually in no position to render help. But both African Americans and whites could and did assist slaves who dared to attempt flight.

Escapes, like all other types of protest, took many forms. Most were impulsive responses to one beating too many, or to the threat of being sold "down the river" to a plantation farther south, where conditions were likely to be more brutal. Such unplanned flights were usually into the swamps and woods near the slave's quarters and did not last long. In some cases, escapees did not even intend to remain free, but hoped that their treatment would improve after they had hidden out for a few weeks. They sought shelter in caves, living on what food they could find or catch or what their friends brought them at night. Owners or professional slave-catchers tracked escapees like wild game, often using specially trained "negro-dogs" to sniff them out. Rewards were offered for their recapture.

There were cases of escaped slaves banding together to form their own colonies, organized to resist white society. Living like guerrilla fighters, they sometimes attacked plantations, stole livestock, and provided a haven to other fugitives. In the lower South and the West Indies, such runaways were called "maroons" (from the Spanish word for "wild"). Nearer the border, where bands of escapees were called "outlyers," fugitives were more likely to try to cross into the North. In Virginia, established communities of maroons, sometimes reaching considerable size, existed as early as the 1650s and represented a serious danger to plantation owners.

In many areas along the Atlantic coast, escaped slaves joined Native Americans, who welcomed them as fellow victims of white oppression. The Indian tribes living in the Virginia and New York colonies agreed to return escaped African slaves, but none ever kept the promise to do so.

Instead, the two peoples formed strong alliances and created stable, prosperous communities.

The runaways who constituted the largest threat to slavery were those who chose to head for the North. There they could attain real freedom and live not as fugitives but as citizens of the country. Few who tried the journey from the Deep South were successful; the forces of nature and white society were too powerful. But slaves in the Upper South states like Virginia, Delaware, Maryland, Kentucky, and Missouri had a better chance to cross over into freedom. It was not easy, and it required great courage and stamina.

It also required ingenuity and a cool head. Douglass passed himself off as a sailor, with borrowed papers, for a perilous boat ride from Delaware to Pennsylvania. Henry Bibb, in trying to free his wife and child, escaped, was recaptured, and escaped again so many times that he became an expert. "Among other good trades I learned the art of running away to perfection," he recalled wryly in his autobiography. "I made a regular business of it, and never gave it up, until I had broken the bands of slavery, and landed myself safely in Canada, where I was regarded as a man and not as a thing."

Among the most daring and adventurous escapes was that of William and Ellen Craft, Georgia slaves who escaped north by the bold means of a disguise. The lighter-skinned Ellen played the part of a male slave owner, her husband that of her black slave. Mrs. Craft wore a man's clothes and a tall hat; to hide her face, she claimed a toothache and covered her mouth with a scarf; to conceal her eyes she wore dark glasses. Her servant-husband made all the arrangements, explaining that his master was too ill to speak. The odd couple stayed in hotels (Mrs. Craft couldn't write and had to claim a sprained hand when told to sign the registers); they bought train tickets, waving aside all questions about their peculiar traveling arrangements; and finally they reached a helpful white organization that was waiting for them in Philadelphia.

*Northern Hospitality—New-York nine months law.* [The Slave steps out of the Slave State, and his chains fall. A Free State, with another chain, stands ready to reenslave him.]

*An illustration from the* American Anti-Slavery Almanac, 1840. (Library of Congress)

Even more ingenious was the escape of Henry "Box" Brown, a Virginia slave possessing unusual skill and nerve. Brown constructed a crate big enough to hold him, and had a white friend ship him as freight to an antislavery organization in Pennsylvania. He carried water and crackers for the trip and waited patiently until the parcel was delivered. When the box was pried open and he was "resurrected," he extended his hand to his anxious rescuers and calmly said, "How do you do, gentlemen?" So successful was "Box" Brown's escape that the white friend who had nailed him into his box and mailed him off repeated the trick for two other slaves. Unfortunately, he was not so successful the third time.

Someone reported him and he was arrested. He spent the next eight years in prison for his kindness.

The Crafts and Henry Brown were among the lucky ones who made it, but more escapes failed than succeeded. The risk was very great. A slave found away from his owner's land without a pass was technically defined as a runaway and could be arrested by any white. In Louisiana, it was legal to shoot a black who did not surrender when challenged by a white. A North Carolina notice described an escaped slave and announced that "any person may KILL and DESTROY the said slave by such means as he or they may think fit, without accusation or impeachment of any crime or offense for so doing."

Worse yet, fugitives were not necessarily free even if they got to a free state. The U.S. Constitution (created to "establish justice" and "secure the blessings of liberty") gave the owners of slaves the right to pursue them into free states and bring them back, with the help of federal forces if necessary. As the value of slaves increased during the 19th century—an unskilled laborer brought an average price of $600 in the 1820s but sold for $1,500 in the 1850s—Southern slaveholders, increasingly determined to hold onto their human property, spared no effort to recover any that slipped away from them.

## Rebellion

The various forms of resistance, from working slowly to running away, persisted throughout the country during the entire period of slavery. They had no real hope of changing or abolishing the system, but more ambitious efforts did occasionally occur. Some slaves planned and organized open rebellions, not merely against their particular masters but against slavery itself.

Such revolts were rare—far rarer in the United States than in the West Indies and South America, where plantations were

# African Americans in the Military _____

Africans Americans have served in the United States armed forces in every war since the Revolution. For some, military service was a way of escaping slavery, but others were prompted by a desire to serve a country they had come to feel was their own.

In 1770, a major confrontation leading to the Revolutionary War took place in front of the Customs House in Boston, when a mob assaulted some British soldiers. The first of five patriots shot during this skirmish was a runaway ex-slave named Crispus Attucks. Both slaves and free African Americans fought in the war that followed. The British cleverly offered freedom to any slave who joined their side. Initially, Congress barred people of African descent, whether free or slave, from joining the American army. But the British were so successful in enlisting slaves seeking their freedom that Congress was forced to lift its ban. After this change in policy it welcomed free African Americans and offered freedom to slaves who would fight for the new nation. Among those who

bigger and slaves usually outnumbered whites. But they did occur, and more frequently than slave owners liked to admit.

Scholars do not agree on how many slave rebellions took place between colonial times and the Civil War. One scholar calculates more than 250 plots and uprisings during that period; others think that the number of incidents was exaggerated by fear among slave owners in the South and by indignation among Northerners who opposed slavery. But history records enough major slave rebellions to establish a pattern and to explain why Southern whites lived in such terror.

## New York, 1712

Of the dozen or so significant uprisings of African Americans before the Revolutionary War, two stand out as especially significant. In April 1712, 25 or 30 slaves, including two enlisted were many free African Americans, including the hero Peter Salem, who turned the tide of battle at Bunker Hill in 1775.

African Americans fought on both sides in the Civil War, but the number drafted into service for the South was small, and many deserted to the North as soon as they had the chance. Like the Revolutionary forces, the Union army was slow to accept African Americans into its ranks, and at first may served unofficially, as spies, medical aides, and laborers. When the North revised its rules, the Union came to welcome the contribution of African-American soldiers and sailors. Many free blacks fought heroically for the cause of national unity and for an end to the institution of slavery.

Although the races sometimes fought side by side during the Revolutionary War, African Americans were officially put in separate units, led by whites. This segregation remained the policy of the United States government in every armed conflict through World War II. It was not until 1948, when President Harry S. Truman signed an order integrating all branches of the military services, that African Americans received the freedom to serve as equals.◆

Native Americans, formed a well-planned and coordinated strike for freedom. They armed themselves with guns, knives, and clubs and set fire to some houses at the northern edge of New York City. Then they barricaded themselves and prepared for a siege. When a group of whites attacked them, the slaves responded by killing nine and wounding five or six others. The colonial army soon arrived and put down the rebellion. Some of the slaves preferred death to surrender: One shot his wife and himself. Four or five others, without guns, cut their own throats. The punishment of those remaining was swift and severe. The government wanted to make a clear example of the rebels to prevent the idea of revolt from spreading to others. Two months after the rebellion, the governor of New York wrote proudly of the state's retribution: of the 21 slaves executed, he reported, "Some were burnt others hanged, one broke on the wheele, and one hung alive in chains in the town, so that there has been the most exemplary punishment inflicted that could be possibly thought of."

## Stono, South Carolina, 1739

Despite this "exemplary punishment" and the clear warning it offered, rebellion did spread. In 1739, in Stono, South Carolina, an even larger confrontation took place. It began when about 20 slaves banded together and attacked the Stono military arsenal. They seized the arms stored there and began a march to Florida, which was then a colony of Spain and was engaged in a war against England. Since they were rebelling against English colonists, the slaves hoped to be welcomed by England's Spanish enemies when they reached the border of Florida. Waving flags, beating drums, and calling out "Liberty," they burned plantations and killed whoever opposed them as they made their way south. Other slaves joined them, and their number reached about 80 by the time the South Carolina militia got word of their march. In the battle that followed—America's largest between slaves and colonists until that time—21 whites and 44 slaves were killed.

## New York, 1740–41

Slaves achieved nothing concrete from the Stono rebellion, and their loss of life far exceeded that of their enemies. Nevertheless, the yearning for liberty was not dampened. Small local outbreaks continued to keep slaveholders nervous throughout the country. In 1740 a rumor circulated in New York City that slaves intended to poison the water supply, so most residents of the city switched to drinking

## NOTES

p. 31 "As the master studies . . ." Frederick Douglass, *My Bondage and My Freedom* (1855; New York: Arno Press, 1969), p. 81.

p. 32 "lay up a month . . ." George Washington, letter to his steward, March 8, 1795, quoted in M. D. Conway, ed., *George Washington and Mount Vernon* (Brooklyn, N.Y.: Long Island Historical Society, 1889), vol. IV, p. 179.

p. 34 "protested publickly that he would not be sold . . ." quoted by Darold D. Wax, "Negro Resistance to the Early American Slave Trade," *Journal of Negro History*, 51 (January 1966), p. 15.

p. 34 "goaded into uncontrollable madness . . ." Solomon Northrup, *Twelve Years a Slave* (1853; Baton Rouge, La.: Louisiana State University Press, 1968), pp. 170–71.

p. 35 "without consultation or deliberation . . ." Frederick Douglass, *Narrative of the Life of Frederick Douglass, an American Slave* (1845; Garden City, N.Y.: Doubleday, 1963), p. 25.

p. 35 "'You had better not!'" James Mars, *Life of James Mars, a Slave Born and Sold in Connecticut* (1869; Miami, Fla.: Mnemosyne, 1969), pp. 24–25.

p. 36 "At that moment . . ." Douglass, p.73.

p. 39 "Among other good trades . . ." Henry Bibb, *Narrative of the Life and Adventures of Henry Bibb, an American Slave* (1850; Salem, N.H.: Ayer, 1991), pp. 15–16.

p. 41 "any person may KILL . . ." quoted in Kenneth M. Stampp, *The Peculiar Institution: Slavery in the Ante-Bellum South* (1956; New York: Vintage Books, 1989), p. 213.

p. 43–44 "Some were burnt others hanged . . ." Governor Robert Hunter to Lords of Trade, quoted in E. B. O'Callaghan, *Documents Relative to the Colonial History of the State of New York* (Albany, N.Y.: 1853–87), vol. 5, pp. 341–42, quoted in Herbert Aptheker, *American Negro Slave Revolts* (New York: International Publishers, 1993), p. 221.

spring water they bought from street vendors. The next year brought a series of unexplained fires. The city's fear and suspicion turned to panic when reports circulated of a conspiracy among New York slaves to burn down the city, kill all the white people, and establish a monarchy for themselves. In a city of 10,000 whites and 2,000 African or African-American slaves, the threat of a widespread insurrection was so terrifying that the government was forced to act promptly to calm the public. Although there was no certain evidence that there really was a conspiracy, witnesses were bribed or tortured to provide names. After a hasty trial, 31 slaves and four white "instigators" were publicly hanged.

> Gentlemen tell us, though hardly think them serious, the people of this descriptic can never systematize a rebellion. . . . Experience speaks a different language
>
>
>
> David Bard, addressing the U.S. House of Representatives, February 14, 1804

New York City breathed a sign of relief, but tension remained in the air. As the Revolutionary War drew near, one way to defuse the danger of slave rebellion was to offer slaves freedom in return for service in the Continental army. Rhode Island drafted two battalions of slaves and paid their owners £120 for each, a high price at the time. Slaves were encouraged to enlist in New Hampshire, Connecticut, New York, and Virginia, and those who did were rewarded by being given their freedom when the war was over. The number of African Americans who served in the Continental army is estimated at 4,000, most of them slaves who were freed after the war.

But the War for American Independence did not produce independence for more than a small percentage of slaves, and the rest still had their own war to wage. The small encounters in New York and Stono had only been skirmishes. Much bigger battles were yet to come.

# 4

# Gabriel: The First Major Attempt

The end of the 18th century was a period of confusion for the United States. The new country, still excited about gaining its independence from England, grew increasingly fearful of internal demands to free slaves. The Revolutionary War had thrown daily life into such disorder that thousands of slaves, in both the North and the South, had broken away from their owners. Some were released to fight in the Continental army. Others joined the British troops. Many simply took advantage of the confusion and ran away. Sometimes the entire slave force of a plantation escaped together: The Virginia plantation of John Willoughby lost all of its 87 slaves at once. One scholar estimates that South Carolina lost 30 percent of its slave population during the Revolution. Many owners were forced to hire their slaves out to others, making it harder to maintain control over them. Plantation slaves now often worked in the cities and met new people, broadening their outlook and experiencing an increased desire for freedom.

New ideas were in the air. The French Revolution of 1789 filled the Western world with talk of liberty and equality. People everywhere heard these ideas and reacted to them. In the French colony of Saint-Domingue—now Haiti—there was a slave revolt in the 1790s on a scale unlike anything yet seen in the United States. It so shook the French army that Napoleon gave up his dream of an empire in America, sold his vast Louisiana Territory to the United States, and pulled out of the New World.

American slaveholders grew understandably alarmed about the influence such events might have among their slaves. They did what they could to prevent West Indian immigrants from entering the United States and spreading ideas of freedom. But American slaves knew all about what was going on in the Caribbean, and rebellion throughout the young country increased steadily. In the first year of the new century there were costly fires of mysterious origin from Georgia and South Carolina all the way to New York and New Jersey. While no one knew for sure who was responsible, many believed they were set by slaves. The postwar disorder continued in the election year of 1800, and with the New York and Stono rebellions still fresh in memory, slave revolt was very much in the air.

Slaves, especially, were thinking about revolt, and the number of mi-

> If something is not done, and soon done, we shall be the murderers of our own children (for) the revolutionary storm, now sweeping the globe, will be upon us.
>
>
>
> Thomas Jefferson, letter to St. George Tucker, August 28, 1791

" *Poor things, ' they can't take care of themselves.'* "

*Southerners often regarded slaves as helpless "children of nature." This ironic picture from an antislavery publication shows how erroneous that image was.* (Library of Congress)

nor incidents of rebellion grew steadily. Then in August of 1800, the details of a carefully planned slave rebellion emerged—one on a larger scale than anything that had yet occurred in the history of North America. If it had succeeded, the history of the American South might have been far different. The rebellion was planned in Richmond, the populous and prosperous capital of Virginia. Some 5,700 people lived in Richmond, more than half of them slaves or free African Americans. Fears of an uprising had been widespread there for months. Then, on August 9, the governor received a letter warning him of a conspiracy. The letter contained no specific information, and it would be three more weeks before the details of the plot became known.

On August 30, a Saturday, two slaves told their master, a wealthy plantation owner named Mosby Sheppard, that a rebellion was scheduled for that night. The leader was a slave they called "General Gabriel."

Gabriel was a huge man—some 6 feet 2 inches tall, according to reports—belonging to Thomas H. Prosser, a local planter known for "behaving with great barbarity to his slaves." Born in the Revolutionary War year of 1776, Gabriel was an expert blacksmith with a reputation for courage and intelligence. According to the two informers, there were several others involved, including Gabriel's wife Nanny and his brothers Solomon and Martin. A slave named Jack Bowler was also involved. An experienced soldier, Bowler had been entrusted with the command of the rebels.

This rebellion was no spontaneous impulse. Since the spring the plotters had been stockpiling swords (produced by Solomon from scythe blades), bayonets, about 500 bullets, and 10 pounds of gunpowder, and had laid careful and exact plans.

The conspirators planned to meet in Henrico County, near Richmond, at Prosser's plantation. They intended to kill Prosser and all his white neighbors and then march to Richmond. Gabriel had mapped out the city and located the storehouses where weapons were kept, and his troops planned to seize them and occupy the city. There they would be able to provide themselves with bread from the mills and money from the treasury.

When Mosby Sheppard heard this frightening information from his slaves, he lost no time in notifying the governor in the nearby capital. The governor of Virginia in 1800 was James Monroe, a lawyer who had studied under Thomas Jefferson and who was later to become the fifth president of the United States. An efficient administrator, he acted swiftly. He posted guards at the federal armory, set up cannon at the capitol building, mustered troops, and placed patrols along the roads from Prosser's house to the city. But that night nature played an unexpected part in the drama: Before dark a furious storm broke out. Reporting the event in a letter to Jefferson, who was then vice president and a candidate for president, a journalist wrote,

> ... upon that very evening just about Sunset there came
> on the most terrible thunder storm, accompanied with

an enormous rain, that I ever witnessed in this State. Between Prosser's and Richmond, there is a place called Brook Swamp which runs across the high road, and over which there was a . . . bridge. By this, the africans were of necessity to pass, and the rain had made the passage impracticable.

The planned invasion had to be called off, but despite the weather about a thousand armed slaves met at the appointed place outside of Richmond. Whether Governor Monroe's precautions would have stopped them if the rain had not prevented the attack remains a question. In the same letter to Jefferson, the witness noted that "they could hardly have failed of success; for after all we could only muster four or five hundred men of whom not more than thirty had Muskets."

Apparently, although the rebels had disbanded during the rain, they intended to regroup and try again. The governor moved promptly during the next three days, ordering the arrest of every slave who might have been connected with the plot. Many were rounded up and brought to trial within the week. As the trials continued during September, more details became known. The public learned to its horror that Gabriel had mobilized support from at least five surrounding counties. He had also made arrangements to recruit the neighboring Catawba tribe of Indians to join in the fight against the whites. We cannot be sure how many slaves were really involved in the conspiracy; different witnesses gave estimates ranging from 2,000 to 6,000. Gabriel himself is quoted as claiming 10,000, and the governor of Mississippi announced that the rebels numbered no fewer than 50,000. According to Governor Monroe, "It was distinctly seen that it embraced most of the slaves in this city and neighborhood . . . ; and there was good cause to believe that the knowledge of such a project pervaded other parts, if not the whole of the state."

In the courtroom during the next few weeks, participants revealed just how carefully and skillfully the rebellion had been planned. "General" Gabriel's army had troups of cavalry and infantry, and military ranks had been assigned to the officers. The attack on Richmond was to begin with slaves setting fire to a section of the city where the houses were all made of wood. While the residents were busy fighting the fire, the rebels planned to seize the penitentiary, the capitol building, and the armory. When they had possession of all the arms and ammunition, they planned to meet the citizens returning from the fire.

The trials revealed more then just how well organized the rebellion was; they also gave chilling evidence of the bitterness and anger that prompted it. According to the testimony of some of the participants, they planned to kill all whites, making exceptions only of Quakers, Methodists, and French people, because those groups opposed slavery. Poor whites without slaves would also be spared because they were expected to join the rebels. According to a newspaper report of October 6, when all the other whites were dead, Gabriel intended to be crowned king of Virginia and to appoint his own government.

The white public was even more horrified to learn that the group had gathered recruits over many months and had found a ready response everywhere. One enlistee, when he was told that he looked too weak to kill a man, replied without hesitation, "Do not take me by my looks. I could kill a white man as free as eat." Another, when first informed of the conspiracy, replied that the slaves should have rebelled a long time ago and assured the recruiter that he would "slay the white people like sheep."

Gabriel himself, and his second-in-command, Jack Bowler, slipped away when the arrests started and remained at large while these sensational trials were going on. Governor Monroe offered a reward of $300 for information leading to their arrest, and a pardon if the informer was connected with the conspiracy. Either fugitive would have been easy to recognize, but perhaps not so easy to apprehend. Gabriel, well above the average height for that period, was missing two front teeth and had several scars on his face; the even more identifiable Bowler was described in the governor's announcement as "a black man about twenty-eight years of age, six feet and four or five inches high, stout and perhaps as strong as any man in the state. He has very long hair for a Negro, which he wears cued behind and twisted on the side. He has a scar over one eye, and is by trade a ditcher."

Gabriel made his way to the docks four miles below Richmond and convinced the captain of the schooner *Mary* to take him on board. There he hid for 11 days, until he was recognized in Norfolk harbor and reported to the police by a slave named Billy who worked on the schooner. Carried back to Richmond in chains on September 24, Gabriel was quickly tried, convicted, and hanged.

The giant Jack Bowler had been hiding in the home of a free African American named Peter Smith, but the news of Gabriel's death crushed his spirit. Two days later, at the urging of his host, he agreed to turn himself in. For persuading him to do so, Smith was credited with bringing him to justice, but when he claimed the $300 reward, the state allowed him only $50. When Billy, the slave who had recognized Gabriel and betrayed him in Norfolk, petitioned for his reward, he too was given only $50. Governor Monroe explained that Billy did not deserve the full amount because he was a slave.

Everyone, slave and free, agreed that the conspirators died well and bravely. Governor Monroe, who in-

> The accused have exhibited a spirit, which, if it becomes general, must deluge the Southern country in blood. They manifested a sense of their rights, and contempt of danger, and a thirst for revenge which portend the most unhappy consequences.
>
>
>
> John Randolph, letter to Joseph Nicholson, September 26, 1800

# Thomas Jefferson and Slavery ─────

The author of the Declaration of Independence, the father of the Bill of Rights, and a two-term president of the United States, Thomas Jefferson was an influential figure in the shaping of American thought and a leading champion of human rights. Yet he himself owned slaves and supported the system of slavery. This contradiction was a source of personal conflict for him as a citizen and of difficulty for him as a statesman.

Jefferson was born in 1743 to one of the richest families in Virginia. He owned some 14,000 acres and over a hundred slaves. At his death in 1826 he freed only five of them (thought to be his own illegitimate children); some of the rest were sold at auction. He was said to have been a kind master, but he never even considered releasing his slaves.

His diaries and published writings show that Jefferson opposed slavery on moral grounds. But although he wrote in the Declaration of

terviewed Gabriel, tried to get him to reveal the names of his accomplices, but Gabriel refused to cooperate and went to his death with dignity. "From what he said to me," Monroe reported sadly, "he seemed to have made up his mind to die, and to have resolved to say but little on the subject of the conspiracy."

There is some dispute about exactly how many members of Gabriel's conspiracy were executed — the newspapers of the time do not agree, and the trials were conducted as secretly as possible. Historians' estimates range between twenty-seven and forty-one, including Gabriel and his two brothers. The law required that a slaveholder be paid for any slave that the state either executed or freed, and thus Virginia was put to great expense by Gabriel's conspiracy. Gabriel himself was valued at $400, a high price at the time, and Mr. Prosser collected it. The two slaves who had reported the conspiracy to Mosby Sheppard—and thus rendered a great

Independence that "all men are created equal," he clearly believed Africans to be naturally inferior and therefore impossible to include in American society. "Nothing is more certainly written in the book of fate," he wrote in his *Autobiography* in 1821, "than that these people are to be free; nor is it less certain that the two races, equally free, cannot live in the same government." He wanted to see the end of slavery, but only on the condition that all people of African descent be deported.

In the Virginia Bill Concerning Slaves, which Jefferson wrote as governor in 1779, any free African American who entered the state could be re-enslaved on sight. No person of color could testify in court in any case to which a white was a party, and freedom of speech and assembly were denied to both free blacks and slaves.

Jefferson realized and was troubled by the inconsistency in his beliefs that slavery was wrong but that it was impossible to allow Africans to be citizens. "We have the wolf by the ears," he wrote in 1821, "and we can neither hold him, nor safely let him go. Justice is in one scale and self-preservation in the other."◆

service to the state—were rewarded by being set free. Their shrewd owner set a price of $500 for each, much more than their market value, but Governor Monroe had no choice under the law but to pay it.

But unwillingness to pay the expenses was not what kept the total number of executions down. Monroe, who had built his political career as a liberal believing in equality, was unwilling to put people to death for fighting for the same belief; and his former teacher, Thomas Jefferson, warned him against being too severe—on practical if not on humanitarian grounds. When a nervous James Monroe wrote asking his advice, Jefferson wrote back advising moderation. "Where to stay the hand of the executioner is an important question," he reminded Monroe, and added, "there is a strong sentiment that there has been hanging enough. The other states and the world at large will forever condemn us if we indulge a principle of revenge, or go one step beyond absolute necessity. They cannot lose sight of the rights of the two parties, & the object of the unsuccessful one."

That object—the life, liberty, and pursuit of happiness guaranteed in the Declaration of Independence—was eloquently stated by one of the prisoners during the trial in Richmond. His words were troubling to whites but inspiring to slaves. Asked what he had to say to the court before being sentenced, he said,

> I have nothing more to offer than what George Washington would have had to offer, had he been taken by the British and put to trial by them. I have adventured my life in endeavoring to obtain the liberty of my countrymen, and am a willing sacrifice to their cause: and I beg, as a favor, that I may be immediately led to execution. I know that you have pre-determined to shed my blood, why then all this mockery of a trial?

The trial and the hangings did not put an end to the Gabriel case. Its memory remained very much alive in the minds of both slaves and their owners. The first consequence

*Slaves continued to be imported long after the slave trade was made illegal.* (New York Public Library Picture Collection)

of the incident was fear among whites, who began locking their doors. The city of Richmond established a public guard that was maintained, at great expense, for half a century. A plan to deport all slaves to Africa became popular, and Governor Monroe conferred with his old friend and fellow Virginian, the newly elected president Thomas Jefferson, about using a part of the recently acquired Louisiana Territory to establish a separate colony in which African Americans could be segregated. New laws further restricted the freedom of slaves, only increasing their anger and frustration. It was a vicious circle—the harder life was made for slaves, the more they rebelled, and the more they rebelled, the harder life was made for them.

In 1802, several small uprisings occurred in Virginia as a direct result of Gabriel's heroic efforts. In April, a conspiracy was discovered that included several of Gabriel's former associates, still carrying on his work. One of Gabriel's recruiters, Sancho, organized a plan to attack on either Good Friday or Easter Monday, both holidays when slaves might gather without arousing the suspicions of their owners. Sancho was determined to profit by Gabriel's mistakes. He kept the plot simple and small in scale in order to reduce the chance of betrayal. Like Gabriel, Sancho intended to begin by burning the town, and he expected more slaves and poor whites to join him when the fight began. But the secret got out, and the Easter conspiracy failed just as Gabriel's had. Nine leaders were arrested, and two of them (including Sancho) were hanged.

Nevertheless, the dream of liberty refused to die. Reports of plots surfaced throughout the country during the next few years. In April 1810, residents of Georgia discovered plans for an insurrection. In May, North Carolina had to take steps to protect itself from rebellion. And in November "a dangerous conspiracy among the negroes" was uncovered in Lexington, Kentucky. These were all small-scale plots, but at the beginning of the next year a really serious rebellion occurred, this time in Louisiana.

The Louisiana Territory had been acquired from France in 1803 and the region was still very disorganized. In addition, news of revolts on the French islands in the West Indies filled everyone's imagination. On January 8, 1811, a force of some 500 men, led by Charles Deslondes, a free mulatto from the Caribbean, began a 35-mile march in organized units toward the city of New Orleans. Armed only with knives, axes, and sticks at first, they attacked the plantation of a Major Andry, killed his son, and took the arms they found there. Then they proceeded from plantation to plantation, increasing in number as slaves joined them along the way.

But their courage and determination were no match for the well-armed forces of the government, which called out the militia and launched a frontal attack on the rebels. Some 400 state militiamen and 260 army soldiers made short work of the rebel forces. Early on the morning of January 10 they cut the slave force to pieces, killing 36, capturing 16 more, and scattering the rest. The captives were tried in New Orleans and all were executed, their heads displayed at regular intervals along the road from the city to Major Andry's plantation as a grim warning to others. It was the beginning of a spiral of heightened slave rebellion, and many considered it part of Gabriel's legacy.

> In this vast march of the mind, the blacks, who are far behind us, may be supposed to advance at a pace equal to our own, but, sir the fact is, they are likely to advance much faster.
>
>
>
> George Tucker, *Letter to a Member of the General Assembly of Virginia, on the Subject of the Late Conspiracy of the Slaves, With a Proposal for Their Colonization* (1801)

## NOTES

p. 50–51 "upon that very evening . . ." James Thomas Callender, letter to Thomas Jefferson, September 13, 1800, quoted in

Herbert Aptheker, *American Negro Slave Revolts* (1943; New York: International Publishers, 1993), p. 221.

p. 51 "they could hardly have failed . . ." Callender, quoted in Nicholas Halasz, *The Rattling Chains: Slave Unrest and Revolt in the Antebellum South* (New York: McKay, 1966), p. 91.

p. 51 "It was distinctly seen . . ." James Monroe to the Speakers of the General Assembly, December 15, 1800, quoted in Stanislaus M. Hamilton, ed., *The Writings of James Monroe* (New York: Putnam, 1898–1903), vol. III, p. 239.

p. 52 "Do not take me by my looks . . ." Executive Papers, September–December, 1800, in the Virginia State Library, Richmond, quoted by Gerald W. Mullin, *Flight and Rebellion: Slave Resistance in Eighteenth-Century Virginia* (New York: Oxford University Press, 1972), p. 145.

p. 53 "a black man about twenty-eight . . ." *Norfolk Herald*, September 8, 1800, quoted in Joseph Cephas Carroll, *Slave Insurrections in the United States, 1800–1865* (1938; New York: Negro Universities Press, 1968), p. 53.

p. 54 "From what he said to me . . ." James Monroe, quoted in Hamilton, vol. III, p. 213.

p. 55–56 "Where to stay the hand of the executioner . . ." Thomas Jefferson, letter to James Monroe, September 15, 1800, in Hamilton, vol. III, p. 208–209.

p. 56 "I have nothing more to offer . . ." A participant in Gabriel's conspiracy, to the court, 1800, quoted in Samuel Sutcliffe, *Travel Through Some Parts of North America in the Years 1804, 1805 and 1806* (Philadelphia: B. & T. Kite, 1812), p. 50.

5

# Encouragement from Outside: The Caribbean Example

T he beginning of the 1800s was a time of trouble in the French and English colonies of the Caribbean, no less than in the newly independent United States. In the islands just off America's southeastern shore, the French Revolution set off shock waves that were felt throughout the New World, and slaves on the huge island plantations were as widely infected by the desire for independence as their American counterparts.

Slave uprisings took place in the Caribbean islands more frequently and on a larger scale than they did in the United

States. This was not because Caribbean slaves had more courage and spirit, but because of their greater numbers. In the United States as a whole in 1800, there were four whites for every African, slave and free; in the South, slaves represented about one third of the population. But in some of the Caribbean islands, slaves outnumbered whites by as much as ten to one.

## Saint-Domingue

The greatest slave revolt in the history of the Western Hemisphere, and the one that most terrified American slave owners, took place in Saint-Domingue, now Haiti, from 1791 to 1804. Originally part of the Spanish colony of Santo Domingo (its name is a French translation), Saint-Domingue was a small French colony occupying the western third of the island of Hispaniola, where Columbus landed in 1492. By the 18th century, its vast sugar plantations had made it the richest colony in the Caribbean and a strategically important port for France. But the agitation for equality that led to the French Revolution in 1789 brought about the same ferment in Saint-Domingue, where conditions were even more favorable for a revolution. Slaves made up more than five sixths of the population of Saint-Domingue, and despite the prosperity of the island, slaves there were among the most overworked and badly treated in the world. Although the birthrate among slaves was high, so many died as a result of the savage cruelty of Saint-Domingue's whites that there was a constant need for new Africans. About 864,000 were imported to the island during the 18th century.

The constant stream of new slaves into Saint-Domingue meant that native African culture was maintained to a far greater extent than in the United States. And unlike the slave population in the United States at the end of the 18th century, more than half of the slaves on the island had been born free in Africa and had not grown up in a world that accepted the idea of slavery. Their African origins also gave them a unified religious background that was different from that of the New World. The practice of voodoo, based on the power of sorcery and charms, remained intact and served as a source of solidarity among slaves and also among fugitives, who kept the dream of independence alive by organizing guerrilla bands and harassing the planters. These insurgents, like their counterparts in the American South, were called maroons. But the maroons of Saint-Domingue were able to form groups both larger and better organized than the ones barely surviving in the swamps of the American Lower South.

A bitter class conflict was another element of the unrest in the French colony. Mulattoes—people of mixed African and white parentage—were technically free but were denied the rights of full citizenship. They could inherit land and could own slaves, but they were not permitted to hold public office. Nevertheless, because they represented almost half the free people in the colony, and because many of them were quite wealthy and well educated, they formed a powerful group. Ideas about liberty and equality were in the air—stirred up by the French Revolution—and the mulattoes demanded their own equality. They argued that the new Assembly of the Revolution in Paris had issued a Declaration of the Rights of Man—a document that said nothing about race but stated simply that all men were equal.

In 1790, a young mulatto agitator, Vincent Ogé, decided to take that declaration literally and announced that mulattoes had been granted full rights as citizens by the French government. When the Saint-Domingue authorities ordered him to stop making such public statements, he sailed to the United States to buy guns for a mulatto army of liberation.

The whites in Saint-Domingue saw Ogé's efforts as a threat to their power. If mulattoes gained all the legal rights of the white ruling class, slaves would soon follow and demand full rights. The colonial governor promptly ordered Ogé's arrest. The young man fled to the Spanish part of the island, but the authorities there immediately turned him over to the French. Ogé was publicly broken on the wheel, and 20 of his associates were hanged.

Although the mulattoes were fighting for their own rights, they did not support the cause of freedom for the slaves. Still, their small and ineffectual effort at revolution lit the fire that brought about that freedom. The martyrdom of Ogé became one more rallying point for the dissatisfaction felt by the vast population of slaves in Saint-Domingue. In the summer of 1791, a revolt broke out in the northern part of the island. It was nothing like those that had come before.

The first abrupt explosion of slave fury shocked the whole Western world. In a month, more than 2,000 whites were killed, and the destruction of property was unprecedented. American newspapers reported the burning of more than 250 sugar plantations and 900 coffee plantations in the area of Cap-François (now Cap-Haïtien), the French stronghold.

Whites, mulattoes, and slaves all fought one another in the confusion. Whites fought to survive. Mulattoes sometimes supported the whites and sometimes the slaves in hopes of having their rights recognized. Slaves attacked their masters both to win freedom and to take revenge. Plantations and sugar refineries belonging to mulattoes were burned to the ground by outraged whites; those owned by whites were destroyed by mulattoes and slaves.

Newspapers charged all three groups with acts of horrible brutality. Whites were taken from their homes by other whites and beheaded for supporting the mulatto cause. A 70-year-old mulatto was tied to the tail of a horse and dragged through the streets until he died. Helpless slave prisoners were publicly beaten to death. White men, women, and children were broken on the wheel by angry slaves to give the masters a taste of their own medicine. According to

"Toussaint Louverture receives a Letter from the First Consul (Napoleon)," illustration from a 19th-century French history of Haiti. (New York Public Library, Schomburg Center for Research in Black Culture)

one account, the slave flag showed "the body of a white infant impaled upon a stake." The slave ranks, increased by large groups of maroons who willingly joined the fight, swept everything before them.

## Toussaint Louverture

During the chaos of those first few months, a leader emerged among the slaves. A middle-aged coachman who stood 5 feet 2 inches tall, François-Dominique Toussaint did not look much like a heroic leader, but those who worked or fought with him recognized his wisdom and saw something magnetic in his personality. Known among his fellow slaves as "the Physician" because of his education—he had taught himself to read and write both French and Latin while working in the plantation stables, and was a trained veterinarian—Toussaint joined the revolution in 1791 and was soon its leader.

The Spanish, long-time enemies of France, took advantage of the revolutionary unrest in Saint-Domingue to attack from Santo Domingo, Spain's part of the island of Hispaniola, and in 1793 Toussaint crossed the border with his troops to join them. From there, he defeated an army of 3,000 French soldiers. The next year, when the government in Paris agreed to abolish slavery in Saint-Domingue, he returned and joined the French army. His disciplined troops repelled invasions from both Spain and England, which had entered the conflict on the Spanish side. So great was his military

> If the re-establishment of slavery in Saint-Domingue came to pass then I declare to you it would be to attempt the impossible. We have known how to face dangers to obtain our liberty, and we shall know how to face death to maintain it.
>
>
>
> Toussaint Louverture, letter to the French government, 1797

skill that the French promoted him to the rank of general.

Among his men Toussaint became known as Louverture, "the Opening," because everything opened before him in battle. Among the former slaves of Saint-Domingue, he was called the Deliverer. A fearless fighter and an excellent strategist, he subdued the Spanish in the eastern end of the island, unified the mulatto-held south and the black-held north, and in 1798 drove the last of the English off the island. In recognition of his abilities, France made him commander-in-chief of the army and lieutenant-governor of the colony.

He proved to be as good an administrator as he had been a soldier. By 1801, he controlled the entire island of Hispaniola and took the title of governor-general. His first act of office was to write a constitution guaranteeing complete racial equality.

When Napoleon took power in France in 1802, Toussaint knew that the free society he was leading was threatened. He sent the emperor a copy of his constitution, but Napoleon refused to endorse it because it challenged the authority of France. Determined to resume full power in what had been France's richest colony, Napoleon sent an army of 22,000 soldiers in 86 ships to reconquer Saint-Domingue. At the head of the troops was the emperor's brother-in-law, General Charles LeClerc.

When LeClerc entered the island, he immediately returned all the plantations to their former white owners and reestablished slavery. But the country had tasted freedom, and its response was to explode once again into violence. Seeing that he could never assume control, LeClerc reversed himself and declared all the people of Saint-Domingue free and equal. Then, with peace restored, he carried out his real mission. Issuing a false invitation to Toussaint to join him for a diplomatic conference on board his ship, LeClerc seized him and placed him in chains. The aged warrior was prevented from seeing anyone, including his wife and children, and was taken to France, where he died in a dungeon the following year.

But Louverture was not defeated. The Opener knew that he had opened something that would not be closed by his death. "In taking me away from my country, you have cut down only the trunk of the tree of black liberty in Saint-Domingue," he told his captor. "That tree will bloom again, for its roots are deep and strong."

## Jean-Jacques Dessalines and Henri Christophe

In fact, the tree of liberty sprang up again sooner than Toussaint might have expected. His generals Jean-Jacques Dessalines and Henri Christophe, both born slaves, continued the fight with renewed ferocity and with greater shrewdness than the arrogant French ever expected. LeClerc attempted to trick Dessalines as he had done Toussaint, but a servant girl warned the black general in African sign language, and the plot failed. Fate too supported the revolutionaries. Yellow fever proved their most valuable ally, carrying off more French soldiers than the combined forces of Saint-Domingue. In the first few months after the French arrived, 14,000 of their soldiers—more than four fifths of the French army, including five generals—died of the disease. Later that same year, the fever claimed LeClerc himself, some months before the death of Toussaint, the man he had betrayed.

For another year the French tried to suppress the revolution in Saint-Domingue, but with no success. Napoleon sent 20,000 new troops as reinforcements, but under the skillful leadership of Dessalines and Christophe, the Saint-Domingue armies prevailed. With nothing but their passion for liberty, this untrained, almost unarmed mob of slaves pulled off the only successful slave revolt on a national scale in the New World. They were also the first army to defeat Napoleon. On November 29, 1803, Dessalines and Christophe

# Slave Rebellion in Latin America _____

African slavery in the Caribbean and South America originated and developed in ways that closely paralleled the system of slavery in the United States. Like the British, the Spanish and Portuguese settled great tracts of land and needed labor to work the mines and the huge sugar and coffee plantations. And just as it had in North America, the native population of South America proved an inadequate labor source.

There were many similarities in the slave systems of the two Americas, but there were important differences, too. Catholic Spain and Portugal imposed stricter laws concerning the treatment of slaves than did Protestant England. The Spanish and Portuguese recognized that even an African had an immortal soul and was worthy of respect as a human being. Despite this difference in attitude, the actual treatment of slaves in Latin America was probably as brutal as in the United States, and the death rate was far higher. There were fewer laws against the freeing of slaves, however. Racial mixing was common, and free Africans had much greater opportunities for social and professional advancement.

issued a declaration of the independence of Saint-Domingue, creating the second independent nation in the Western Hemisphere and the first free black republic in the world. Dessalines declared himself Emperor Jean-Jacques I on January 1, 1804, and changed the new nation's name to Haiti—a native word for high place. Two years later he was assassinated by order of Henri Christophe, who ruled as King Henri until his suicide in 1820.

## Jamaica

The new republic of Haiti had suffered a chaotic beginning, with political and social unrest at all levels of society. Nevertheless, its example of successful slave revolution served as

The most important difference between Latin American and British slaves was their relative numbers. Africans outnumbered whites in all Spanish and Portuguese colonies from the beginning. This resulted in higher numbers of slave revolts, and more successful ones. In 1530 a band of Colombian slaves destroyed the town of Santa Marta, and in 1552 a force of 800 took over a mining district in Venezuela. There were also major revolts in Mexico in 1546, 1570, 1608, and 1670. In the 17th century, a group of fugitives formed a maroon colony in Brazil. It was recognized as an independent black republic and lasted for a century.

In the important Brazilian city of Bahia, eight large-scale rebellions took place between 1807 and 1835, mounted by Afro-Brazilians of different tribal backgrounds. The last of these came very close to success, and the Portuguese needed to organize a massive military response to put it down. According to a modern scholar, Bahia came close to becoming another Haiti.

Most of the rebellions in Latin America were no more successful than those in the United States, despite their greater resources of manpower. But like their northern counterparts, they sustained the spirit of independence that ultimately led the way to freedom.◆

a great encouragement to the rest of the Caribbean for many years to come. By the end of the 1820s, slave revolt had become almost universal in the area. Cuba, Puerto Rico, Antigua, Tortuga, and French Martinique (where Napoleon had succeed in reintroducing slavery) were all in a state of rebellion. But none of these islands had conditions more threatening to slave owners than the British colony of Jamaica.

The ratio of slaves to whites in Jamaica was among the highest in the area, and conditions among the worst. When a rumor spread in 1831 that the king of England had declared them free, the 300,000 slaves demanded that his order be carried out. The colonial rulers, representing no more than 30,000 whites, refused to listen to the slaves' demands and punished those who dared to make them. But the time for such arrogant treatment of slaves had come to an end in the

Caribbean. The many stories of rebellion in North and South America sustained their hopes, and the thrilling example of Haiti gave them a new vision of what they could accomplish. In January 1832, some 50,000 Jamaican slaves backed up their demands with force.

It was not a planned, organized military action, but it was still a devastating one. Almost unanimous, the revolt took the form of mass destruction. Houses and sugarcane fields, refineries and rum distilleries, all burned well in the clear Jamaica air, and within days much of the island's industry and more than 150 of its plantations were in ashes.

The British government responded promptly and decisively. The island militia, some 18,000 strong, was joined by the national army, and the governor used warships to land troops along the coast. Declaring a state of national emergency, the government even called on freight and passenger vessels to help in the fight. Spain and the United States sent ships to support the British government, recognizing the danger a successful slave uprising in Jamaica would pose in their own countries.

## Maroons

Jamaica had a long history of slave escapes, and its maroon colonies were large and well established. It was estimated that in 1800 there were over 10,000 fugitives at large in

Jamaica. Slaves who come from the same areas of Africa organized themselves into villages and spoke their original languages, maintaining the social structures and religions of their homelands. Over many generations, they developed stable societies with clearly defined African cultures intact. Skillful guerrilla warriors who knew the jungles and mountains better than the English settlers, the maroons were almost impossible to conquer. Over the years, the largest of these maroon bands became more or less official communities. They were recognized by the English and left alone to raise their own crops and live their own lives. Some entered into treaties with the planters and did business with them.

The survival of these maroon colonies depended on their cooperation with the English. No longer fugitives, the descendants of escaped Spanish and English slaves lived in towns built on land the government had turned over to them. During the slave uprising of 1832, maroons lent their support to the government. As loyal citizens, they willingly fought for the English against the rebelling slaves.

The combination of well-equipped military force, foreign support, and maroon cooperation was too much for the slaves, and their insurrection was crushed. As in most slave rebellions, the rebels lost more than their enemies did: Fewer than 15 whites lost their lives compared with some 400 rebels killed in the fighting and around 100 executed afterward. But the fruits of English victory were not to last. Resistance so desperate and persistent made it clear that slavery could no longer be profitably imposed by force. Even though the slaves were defeated, their revolt proved to be the last straw for the colony. The effort to maintain a slave economy in the Caribbean had cost England many lives and more money than their West Indian colonies were bringing in. For years antislavery organizations such as the Quakers had been pressuring the government to end slavery on moral and spiritual grounds. The 1832 rebellion made it obvious that there were good practical and financial reasons to do so as well. The rebels lost the battle, but ultimately won the war when Britain ended slavery in its colonies in 1833.

## Caribbean Rebellion and United States Slave Resistance

News of slave uprisings in the Caribbean had a profound impact on thought in the United States. The initial response among whites in the South was sympathy for the "victims," but in time slave owners began to be increasingly alarmed at the possibility of the same thing happening on their own shores. The discovery of Gabriel's conspiracy in Virginia gave those fears additional weight.

There is no evidence that Gabriel was directly influenced by the events in Saint-Domingue, but it is clear that the same spirit influenced both rebellions. The slaveholding class feared the effect of such ideas, but it feared direct personal influence even more. Rumors were common throughout the 1790s that agents of the Caribbean revolution were slipping into the United States to infect American slaves with the germ of revolt, and that a plot was brewing to lend military support to slave insurrections in the United States. Efforts were made to keep West Indian immigrants out of the United states and to censor news about the uprisings that were taking place.

Fears among the whites were not limited to isolated Southern planters, but were common among people in the state governments as well. As early as 1782, some Southern states banned the entry of African refugees from the islands, and after the success of the Saint-Domingue revolt the fear deepened. Slave owners knew the danger of a confrontation; the Gabriel affair showed that slave anger and hatred in the

United States had a short fuse, and that it would not take much to ignite it. The United States did business with Haiti, but it did not recognize the black nation politically for more than 50 years after Haitian independence. The slave-owning states of the South felt that recognizing Haiti would put the stamp of national approval on slave rebellion. As a senator from Georgia put it in 1825, such recognition would "introduce a moral contagion" into our country.

Agitation by the free citizens of Haiti—a nation founded by rebellious slaves—was every slave owner's worst nightmare. A member of the House of Representatives from Virginia, Daniel Sheffey, warned that America might face "the fate of Santo Domingo" (as Saint-Domingue was commonly called in the United States) if it did not maintain constant vigilance against this threat. He reminded his audience that "if ten thousand men landed on Southern shores" with arms for the slaves, "every man would find in his own family an enemy ready to cut the throats of his wife and children."

The end of slavery in Saint-Domingue and Jamaica also had a powerful effect on antislavery forces in the North. To them, the fall of white rule in the Caribbean was proof of the correctness of their position and a warning of the firestorm to come in the United States. They made a great hero of Toussaint, comparing him with George Washington as the bringer of freedom to his people and the father of his country, while Gabriel was portrayed as a martyr for liberty and justice. Magazines were filled with predictions that the United States would experience the same explosion of fury as Saint-Domingue had if slavery were not abolished. In 1801, the year after Gabriel was hanged, a Boston periodical carried a poem warning

> . . . remember ere too late.
> The tale of St. Domingo's fate.
> Tho *Gabriel* dies, a host remain

Oppres'd with slavery's galling chain.
And soon or late the hour will come
Mark'd with Virginia's dreadful doom.

If those opposed to slavery were excited by the success of Caribbean slave rebellions, the slaves themselves experienced a deeper emotion. Although Southern whites did all they could to keep the news hidden, they did not succeed—too many slaves were able to read newspapers, and word spread rapidly. Haiti and Jamaica became models of African courage and strength. Toussaint Louverture was the Opener in the United States as well as in Saint-Domingue. He opened the minds of American slaves to the possibility of winning their own freedom.

## NOTES

p. 67  "In taking me away . . ." Toussaint Louverture, in captivity on board the French ship *Héros*, 1802, quoted in John W. Vandercook, *Black Majesty: The Life of Christophe, King of Haiti* (1928; Garden City, N.Y.: Garden City Publishing, 1950), p. 70.

p. 73  "if ten thousand men landed . . ." Daniel Sheffey, Virginia representative to the U.S. House of Representatives, January 1813, quoted in James Hugo Johnston, *Race Relations in Virginia and Miscegenation in the South, 1776–1860* (Amherst, Mass.: University of Massachusetts Press, 1970), p. 77.

p. 73–74  ". . . remember ere too late . . ." *New England Palladium*, January 6, 1801.

# 6

# *Denmark Vesey: The Revolution That Almost Happened*

Amerıcan slaves developed a remarkable communication system. Despite efforts to keep them from learning to read, and to limit their reading to the Bible if they somehow managed to learn, slaves were able to find out about important events within days of their occurrence. Rebellions in the Caribbean were known to slaves throughout the South, and they were a subject of burning interest. A quiet middle-aged carpenter in Charleston, South Carolina with the strange name of Denmark Vesey took a particular interest in these events. What Vesey did with his

**75**

interest changed the path of American history and nearly started a revolution.

Vesey's background was different from that of the other leaders of American slave resistance. The details of his origin are unknown. Some believe he was born in Africa around 1767 and enslaved while still a child. He grew up in the West Indies on St. Thomas, a Danish island that grew sugar and cotton but depended on slave trading for most of its income. At the age of 14, the boy was purchased by Joseph Vesey, an American slave trader, and transported to Saint-Domingue for sale.

There are two versions of how he got the name Denmark: Some say that Captain Vesey named him Télémaque—the French spelling of Telemachus, the son of Ulysses in Greek mythology. Slave owners considered it a good joke to name their helpless property for heroes of classical antiquity, and slave lists are full of Caesars, Pompeys, and Scipios. The name Télémaque may then have been mispronounced Denmark by other slaves. Other scholars believe that the young slave was given that nickname because he came from St. Thomas, a colony of Denmark.

A boy of unusual intelligence and good looks, he sold easily and for a good price at Cap-François. He then spent a season there, working on a plantation and adding French to the Danish and English he already spoke fluently. Another slave in Saint-Domingue at the time was a lad two years younger named Henri. In little more than 20 years this Henri—Henri Christophe—would lead a revolution and become king of Haiti.

Denmark did not stay in Saint-Domingue for long. Within a year his owner returned him to Captain Vesey as unfit for service because he suffered from epileptic fits. A likable and willing worker, he remained with the captain for the next 20 years, assisting him in transporting and selling slaves. Captain Vesey gave up seafaring in 1783, becoming a slave merchant in Charleston, South Carolina, and Denmark continued as his servant.

Those who knew him—including Captain Vesey—agreed that Denmark was always a loyal slave. He was well treated and seemed reasonably contented. But in 1800—the year Gabriel conspired to overthrow slavery and was hanged for it—things changed abruptly for Denmark. He won a public lottery prize of $1,500. He purchased his freedom from Captain Vesey for $600—much less than the market value of such a capable slave. With the remaining $900 he opened his own carpentry shop.

African-American carpenters earned only $1.50 a day in the early 1800s (white ones received $2.50 for the same work), but Denmark did well and invested his money wisely. By the time he was in his fifties, he was worth over $8,000. Denmark was literate in several languages and well versed in the Bible, and he kept himself informed by reading all the local newspapers. Of the thousand or so free African Americans in Charleston in 1800, Denmark Vesey was among the wealthiest and most respected.

Vesey married often. According to the records, he had a total of seven wives during his life, sometimes more than one at the same time, and he was the father of many children. All his wives were slaves, and it especially galled him that he could only visit them at night with the permission of their owners. His children too were slaves, because a child of a slave mother was born into slavery, the property of its mother's owner, to sell as the owner saw fit.

We have an unusually clear picture of the growing anger Vesey felt. Though now a free man, and one of substance, he was still prevented by law from exercising his full freedom, simply because he was black. Several people who knew him recalled his behavior and the open way he spoke out against injustice. One white witness recollected how he always turned the conversation to the subject of slavery and complained of the laws that subjugated his people. Even in the

*Supporters of slavery argued that the institution conferred a benefit on slaves. This 19th-century cartoon makes fun of that attitude.* (Culver Pictures, Inc.)

company of whites, he praised the revolutionary leaders of Haiti, and when he saw African Americans behaving humbly he would become angry. Once he asked someone why he had bowed to a white man. "Because I am a slave," the other replied. "You deserve to be," Denmark Vesey replied contemptuously.

Another slave recalled a passionate speech Vesey gave in his home. "I have heard him say that the negro's situation was so bad he did not know how they could endure it," the slave reported, "and was astonished that they did not rise and fend for themselves. . . . Vesey said the negroes were living such an abominable life, they ought to rise."

Sometime around 1818, the frustrations of Denmark Vesey's life became too much to bear, and he began to plan an uprising. Inspired by events in Haiti, which he followed very carefully in the daily papers, Vesey determined to follow the example of Toussaint Louverture. But Charleston was not Cap François. The people Vesey sought to free did not make up a vast majority in the city, and they were not able to gather to hear him speak.

However, for several years, African Americans had been allowed their own religious house of worship in a Charleston suburb. What later became the African Methodist Episcopal Church was then a small gathering place where slaves congregated on Sundays. Vesey saw that these meetings would give him a chance to address groups of African Americans and to look for officers to serve in the army he planned to form to overthrow the white government.

He became a favorite preacher in the church. His sermons were eloquent—the passion he felt communicated itself in his powerful voice—and he never failed to include the subject of slavery. Comparing his people to the enslaved Israelites, he reminded his listeners of God's promise of liberation. A favorite text was Zechariah 14:1—"Behold the day of the Lord cometh . . . and the city shall be taken," and he often read from Exodus 2:23–24—"And the children of Israel sighed by reason of the bondage . . . And God heard their groaning, and God remembered his covenant." Vesey intended to kill all the whites in Charleston, and to justify this he quoted the passage "and they utterly destroyed all that was in the city, both men and women, young and old, and ox, and sheep, and ass, with the edge of the sword" (Joshua 6:21).

Vesey planned his rebellion patiently and methodically, and with great insight into the minds of his followers. In addition to citing the Bible to support his case, he called on African traditions, linking his enterprise with the ancient gods of Africa as well as with the god of the Christians. He also quoted extensively from the news of the day, picking his reports carefully to convince his listeners that they would receive help from Haiti when the time came.

Vesey also chose his commanders shrewdly. He picked leaders who represented different native peoples to demonstrate the unity of African identity. Monday Gell, a highly educated harness maker, was an Ibo; Mingo Harth, assigned to serve as a leader of a cavalry troop, was a Mandingo; and Jack Pritchard, known as Gullah Jack—a revered sorcerer believed to be able to make people invincible—was an Angolan. Each led a company of his own ethnic group in maneuvers that stressed cooperation among all the rebels. Vesey also chose his soldiers from a wide range of social and professional classes: Ned, Rolla, and Bateau Bennett were personal slaves of the governor of the state, and Vesey included preachers and craftsmen as well as common laborers.

Vesey's plans went beyond Charleston. He appointed Gullah Jack, Monday Gell, and others as agents to enlist the slaves in the plantations outside the city. His reach even extended beyond the borders of the country. Monday Gell, the scribe of the conspiracy, wrote letters to the president of Haiti telling him of the suffering of American slaves and asking for the Haitian people's help. The letter was shrewdly smuggled out of the country and into Haiti by a cook aboard a Northern schooner.

Denmark Vesey's home—a comfortable private house secure from unexpected visits—became a meeting place for his followers and a warehouse for the arms he began collecting. A blacksmith in the group made some 300 daggers and 250 bayonets. Vesey knew that on his own he could never gather enough weaponry to match the resources of the white community, but he knew the city well and he made accurate and detailed maps pinpointing the location of firearms. With these arms, which he intended to seize at the very beginning of the revolt, he hoped he could entrench his forces before the state militia could be summoned.

By 1821, Vesey had given up carpentry and was devoting all his time to recruiting soldiers for his army of revolution. His arguments were subtle but effective. A slave named Bacchus Hamnett remembered in detail how Vesey drew him into agreement with his plans by means of a series of questions, and reported the conversations as follows:

> *Did his master use him Well*—Yes, he believed so, *Did he eat the same as his master*— . . . sometimes not as well as his master—*Did his master not sleep in a soft bed*, Yes. *Did he Bacchus sleep on as soft a bed as his master*—No—*Who made his master*—God—*Who made you*—God—*And then ar'nt you as good as your master if God made him and you, ar'nt you as free*, yes, *then why don't you join and fight your master. . . . Does he whip you when you do wrong*, Yes sometimes, *Then why don't you . . . turn about and fight for yourself.*

With his army and his plan in place, Vesey set the date and time of the attack—June 16, 1822, at the fifth stroke of midnight. The date picked was a Sunday, the same day of the week Gabriel had chosen for his rebellion, because Sunday was the day on which African Americans could gather in the

# Fugitive Slave Laws _____

The United States Constitution, ratified in 1791 after four years of government debate, did not directly support slavery. But it clearly recognized that individual states had the right to maintain the slave system. Its fourth Article included a paragraph authorizing the recapture of slaves that had escaped to states where slavery was illegal. This paragraph stated that such slaves must be "delivered up" to their masters. Two years after the Constitution went into effect, Congress clarified that provision by enacting the Fugitive Slave Law of 1793—one of the most controversial laws the government ever passed.

As Northern opposition to slavery increased during the 19th century, the Fugitive Slave Act increasingly came under attack. Many Northern states passed laws to guarantee personal liberty. These ordinances made the recapture of fugitive slaves difficult and added to the growing tension between Southern state governments and the national government. To support slave owners, Congress passed a second and much stronger fugitive slave law in 1850.

city without being suspected. Also, Vesey had observed that in the heat of summer many whites left the city, so it would be poorly defended.

The time was chosen because there wouldn't be many people on the street at that hour. The plan called for the rebels to attack simultaneously in several places, and, also like Gabriel, they planned to set fires to distract the citizens. Then they would empty the city's gunsmith shops. A group under Rolla was to meet at the governor's mill, put the governor and those around him to death, and march to a bridge linking Charleston with Cannonborough. By fortifying that bridge, they would prevent reinforcements from entering the city. Each of the leaders had a specific assignment—one was to secure supplies, another was to capture arms, yet another was to lead an attack on the guardhouse. A cavalry regiment

This second law increased the power of the state governments to pursue and capture escaped slaves, and denied suspected fugitives the right to a trial. It required private citizens to help hunt down escapees, and made anyone aiding a runaway liable to six months' imprisonment and a $1,000 fine.

The Fugitive Slave Law of 1850 outraged the North. The New England philosopher Ralph Waldo Emerson wrote of it, "This filthy enactment. . . . I will not obey it, by God!" and many Northerners who had not cared much about the issue until then agreed with him. The day after the law was declared, a mob stormed a courthouse in Boston to rescue a recaptured fugitive slave. A batallion of U.S. artillery and four platoons of marines had to be called out to escort the prisoner to the boat waiting to carry him back to his master. That day alone, it cost the government some $40,000 to enforce its new law.

The South saw the fugitive slave laws as necessary to protect their property; the North saw them as an intolerable attack on human liberty and called them the "Man-Stealing Laws" and the "Bloodhound Bills." Before they were repealed, they helped turn many Northerners against the institution of slavery.◆

was formed to patrol the streets and prevent whites from gathering. Any white showing himself outside was to be killed. The plan was organized with considerable strategic skill and with ferocious singleness of purpose. The backup, in case of failure, was to rob the banks and set sail for Haiti.

As carefully as these strategies were developed, there remained the danger of discovery in advance. The betrayal of Gabriel by a slave was common knowledge, and Vesey and his officers took special precautions to avoid a repetition of that calamity. No one was entrusted with more information than he needed for his particular assignment, and even many of the leaders did not know the full plan of action or the identity of the others. No drinkers or excessively talkative people were allowed in the organization. Women were excluded both because they were not trusted to keep the secret and so that they would be saved to take care of the children if the men were defeated. All participants were specifically warned not to discuss the plan with house servants who received gifts from their masters, because these men were especially likely betrayers. Above all, Vesey chose his top command with special care, picking people he knew he could depend on. And he chose well. Peter Poyas, the next in command after Vesey, commanded a company of 600, not one of whom was ever tried in court. To this day no one knows exactly how many people were involved in the planned insurrection or how far it was to extend. Estimates place the number of participants at from 3,000 to 9,000 and the range at some 80 miles around Charleston. We will probably never know the exact details, because white authorities released little information to the press. And the leaders remained sternly silent to the end, even under torture.

But despite the cunning, the care, and the iron discipline of Denmark Vesey and his group, the plan did leak out. A word to the wrong man—ironically, a house slave of exactly the type Vesey had warned of—was all it took. This house slave, informed on May 25 of the uprising planned for June 16, told his master at once. A white society already jumpy because of the Caribbean insurrections quickly organized a defense. On the night of June 16, Charleston was surrounded by a well-armed guard, patrols marched in the major streets, and the conspiracy collapsed. In the next few days, about 100 suspects were rounded up. Vesey hid in the home of one of his wives, but he was arrested there on the 21st.

Only two of the leaders, Monday Gell and Governor Bennett's slave Rolla, confessed. The rest said nothing. Peter Poyas, in chains in a prison cell, called out to a fellow prisoner who showed signs of weakening under torture, "Die silent, as you shall see me do."

The trials took place within days, before a panel of judges but without a jury. Of the 131 men arrested, 35 were sentenced to death and hanged, including all the leaders. The chief magistrate made a solemn speech, full of lofty virtue, when he sentenced Vesey:

> Denmark Vesey—the Court, on mature consideration, have pronounced you Guilty. . . . the Court were not only satisfied of your guilt, but that you were the author and original instigator of this diabolical plot. Your professed design was to trample on all laws, human and divine; to riot in blood, outrage, rapine, and conflagration, and to introduce anarchy and confusion in their most horrid forms. Your life has become, therefor, a just and necessary sacrifice, at the shrine of indignant Justice. . . . To that Almighty Being alone, whose Holy Ordinance you have trampled in the dust, can you now look for mercy. . . .

and so on at great length. Vesey, like his commanders, went to the gallows without a word.

The death of Denmark Vesey and his colleagues did not reassure the whites of South Carolina, but it gave them some idea of what they needed to do to protect themselves from such a conspiracy happening in the future. Though Vesey's rebellion, like that of Gabriel, never actually occurred, it was an important event in the history of Charleston. One contemporary pamphleteer wrote an elaborate explanation of the affair, outlining what he considered its principal causes. Since the trial was full of references to the successful rebellion in the Caribbean, the first cause he listed was "The example of San Domingo [Saint-Domingue], and (probably) the encouragement received from thence." Others included the enthusiastic talk about universal liberty in the North, and the "Idleness, and dissipation, and improper indulgencies permitted among all classes of Negroes in Charleston . . . ; and, as the most dangerous of those indulgencies, their being taught to read and write."

There wasn't much that white Southerners could do about the discussions of antislavery ideas that were taking place in the North, but they could do something about the other dangers to their slave system. In response to the Vesey conspiracy, most Southern states restricted religious gatherings, because churches could be centers for plotting. And the law in South Carolina required that every free African American over the age of 15 have a guardian, and prohibited any free African American who left the state from ever returning.

But of all the many restrictions the South placed on the lives of its African populace, the one that had the farthest-reaching consequences was one designed to prevent exposure of its slaves to contamination from the Caribbean. As one modern scholar has written, "If all free Negroes were regarded by the South as a dangerous species, those from the island of Santo Domingo, where the Africans had revolted, killed the white planters, defeated one of Napoleon's armies and set up a Negro state, were classed with cholera germs."

The state of South Carolina had long tried to isolate its slaves from news about or contact with Haiti, and in reaction to the Vesey case it passed a law forbidding any black or mulatto serving on a ship to enter the state. As soon as a vessel arrived at a South Carolina port, any black, of whatever nationality, and whether slave or free, was to be taken off and

> $P_{oor}$ South Carolina! . . . She has lost her better judgment. . . . She still clings, with unabated love, to the cause of her shame, her misery, and her degradation.
>
>
>
> Hinton Rowan Helper,
> The Impending Crisis of the South:
> How to Meet It (1857)

The Negro Pew, or "Free" Seats for black Christians. | Mayor of New-York refusing a Carman's license to a colored Man.

In both North and South, free African Americans suffered from discrimination, as this illustration from a 19th-century antislavery publication shows. (Library of Congress)

imprisoned until the ship departed. The ship's master was required to pay the jail costs, and if he failed to do so he was to be fined $1,000 or be jailed himself, and the black was to be sold as a slave.

The law, known as the Negro Seaman Act, was challenged as a violation of an American treaty with Great Britain, and was declared unconstitutional in United States federal court. But the senate of South Carolina defied the government and enforced it anyway. This put the nation in what one historian has described as "the humiliating position of explaining to the British Government that the United States could neither control South Carolina nor honor its own treaties." And there were worse consequences yet: The example of a state refusing to conform to the Constitution was contagious. In 1842 Louisiana passed a similar law, and in 1845 Florida became a state with a constitution that refused to admit free African Americans.

This attempt by the South to draw a curtain around itself to protect slaves from the infection of freedom had important historical consequences for the country. Denmark Vesey did not succeed in freeing the slaves, or even in improving their condition, but his action helped drive one more wedge between the white masters of his state and the national government. With his failed rebellion, the nation moved one step closer to the inevitable conflict that would decide the question once and for all.

## NOTES

p. 79  "I have heard him say . . ." Frank, a slave belonging to Mrs. Ferguson, 1822, quoted in Robert S. Starobin, *Denmark Vesey: The Slave Conspiracy of 1822* (Englewood Cliffs, N.J.: Prentice-Hall, 1970) pp. 31–32.

p. 81  "Did his master use him Well . . ." Bacchus Hamnett, a slave, quoted in Starobin, pp. 64–65.

p. 85  "Denmark Vesey—the Court, on mature consideration . . ." Lionel H. Kennedy and Thomas Parker, *An Official Report of the Trials of Sundry Negroes, Charged with an Attempt to Raise an Insurrection in the State of South Carolina* (1822), Quoted in John Lofton, *Denmark Vesey's Revolt: The Slave Plot That Lit a Fuse to Fort Sumter* (1964; Kent, Ohio: Kent State University Press, 1983), pp. 161–62.

p. 85–86  "The example of San Domingo . . ." Achates (Thomas Pinckney), *Reflections Occasioned by the Late Disturbances in Charleston* (1822), quoted in Joseph Cephas Carroll, *Slave Insurrections in the United States, 1800–1865* (1938; New York: Negro Universities Press, 1968), p. 105.

p. 86  "If all free Negroes . . ." Nathaniel Weyl, *The Negro in American Civilization* (Washington, D.C.: Public Affairs Press, 1960), p. 59.

# 7

# Nat Turner:
# The Prophet

The Gabriel and Denmark Vesey rebellions both failed for the same reasons. Although carefully and intelligently planned, they developed over such long periods of time and included so many people that they could not be kept secret. Both were city-based and dependent on the cooperation of urban slaves who were exposed to a wide range of experiences and social contacts. It is not remarkable that these conspiracies, each involving thousands of participants, were betrayed; the surprising thing is that they came as close to success as they did.

The reprisals that followed these conspiracies did not suppress the yearning for equality among African Americans, but there were to be no more attempts at large-scale slave uprisings. Nine years after Denmark Vesey was hanged, however, the South experienced another rebellion. It was small and had no political objectives. It was led by a field hand who had no clearly defined plan, little preparation, almost no weapons, and only six companions. Yet the Nat Turner revolt of 1831 was the bloodiest in American history, and it proved what the others had only suggested: that slaves were willing and able to fight together against the system.

This third and last significant slave uprising in the United States took place in an area of small farms in Southampton County, Virginia, about 150 miles from the nation's capital. Its leader was a man considered a model of loyal, obedient service by his owners. Nat Turner was born among the slaves of Benjamin Turner in 1800, the same year Gabriel met his death and Denmark Vesey bought his freedom. The son of recently imported Africans, Nat Turner had an intensely religious grandmother. His father escaped to Canada when Nat was a child and later returned to Africa.

Young Nat impressed others as extraordinary from the start. He taught himself to read and write at an early age, and his mother reported that he remembered things that had happened before his birth. People predicted that he would be a prophet, and his parents agreed, saying that he was "intended for some great purpose."

He impressed his owners, too. He never lied or stole, neither smoked nor drank, and was devoted to prayer. Although he had no formal religious training he became a Baptist minister. Known among his fellow slaves as the Prophet, he was permitted unusual freedom to travel through the county and preach. He claimed that as he plowed the field one day "the spirit that spoke to the prophets in ancient days" spoke to him and confirmed his belief that he had a divine mission. Several years later, in 1825, he had a vision. As he later described it:

> I saw white spirits and black spirits engaged in battle, and the sun was darkened—the thunder rolled in the Heavens, and the blood flowed in streams—and I heard a voice saying, "Such is your luck, such you are called to see, and let it come rough or smooth, you must surely bear it."

Other signs appeared—drops of blood on the corn, figures and numbers written in blood on leaves—and he was convinced that the day of judgment was at hand, the day when he should "fight against the Serpent, for the time was fast approaching when the first should be last and the last should be first."

He waited for a sign in the heavens that he should "commence the great work," and when an eclipse of the sun occurred in February 1831, he was ready. He recruited four friends and they agreed to act. They first chose Independence Day to declare their own independence—"It was intended by us to have begun the work of death on the 4th of July," he revealed in his confession—but Turner fell ill and they decided to postpone the attack until the next month. In August another heavenly sign appeared: The sun rose a pale greenish color that changed to blue and then to silver. This time there could be no doubt.

On Sunday, August 21, Nat and six others met in the woods to devise a plan, because they had not yet decided exactly what they were going to do. Two of them were new to the group, and Nat asked one, a six-foot-tall slave named Will, why he was there. The property of a cruel man who had sold the slave's wife and scarred his back with whip marks, Will answered that his life was worth no more than those of others and that liberty was as dear to him as to anyone else. "I asked him," Turner reported later, "if he

A 19th-century artist's rendering of the capture of Nat Turner, from Popular History of the United States *by William Cullen Bryant and Sidney Howard Gay, 1876–1880.* (New York Public Library, Schomberg Center for Research in Black Culture)

thought to obtain it? He said he would, or lose his life." That answer was enough to satisfy the rebel leader.

The little band talked until two in the morning and settled on a course of action: They would attack a farm, kill everyone there, and move on to the next farm, collecting weapons, horses, and slave support as they went. All whites they met were to be killed. "Until we had armed and equipped ourselves, and gathered sufficient force," Nat explained, "neither age nor sex was to be spared." They decided to begin that very night, since most of the white men in the area were at a religious meeting across the North Carolina line, leaving their houses unprotected. The first farmhouse they would enter would be that of Nat Turner's owner.

Turner had been sold the year before to a Mr. Joseph Travis, who had treated him very well. Travis was, the slave admitted, "a kind master, and placed the greatest confidence in me; in fact, I had no cause to complain of his treatment to me." But the Prophet's mission was clear, and he could make no exceptions. He agreed to draw first blood. Armed with a hatchet and an axe—all the weapons the little band had been able to obtain in advance—they entered the Travis house and murdered Travis and his family. In his confession, Turner coolly described the event in precise detail:

> I entered my master's chamber, it being dark, I could not give a death blow, the hatchet glanced from his head, he sprang from the bed and called his wife, it was his last word, Will laid him dead, with a blow of his axe, and Mrs. Travis shared the same fate, as she lay in bed. The murder of the family, five in number, was the work of a moment, not one of them awoke; there was a little infant sleeping in a cradle, that was forgotten, until we had left the house and gone some distance, when Henry and Will returned and killed it; we got here four guns that would shoot, and several old muskets, with a pound or two of powder.

The troop continued for the next two days almost unopposed. With no particular destination in mind, they marched from farm to farm, sparing no one with a white skin except one family that was described by a contemporary source as "so wretched as to be in all respects on a par with them." One house held a woman and 10 children; all were killed. A few slaves tried to protect their masters, but most joined the marauders, and in a short time the band had increased to about 60. Now armed with guns, swords, axes, and scythes, and many of them now on horseback, they swept all before them. Although most of their victims were women, there were no sexual assaults. In the three or four days it lasted, Nat Turner's revolt took the lives of about 57 whites and extended about 20 miles from the scene of its first action.

The insurrection ended almost as abruptly as it began. As limited as communication was in that backwater area, the alarm was given within hours. A small group of armed whites attacked the insurgents and wounded several of them. The rebel group scattered, and some returned to their homes, while others continued fighting. Within days, the news had spread so widely that troops from Richmond, Norfolk, and as far away as North Carolina were marching to the area.

Few new recruits joined the rebel band at this stage. The 20 remaining insurgents attacked the house of Dr. Simon Blunt on August 23. In this last battle the rebels were met with armed resistance not only from Blunt and his family but from the doctor's slaves, who fought with farm tools to protect their master. When the militia reached the scene, the rebels were outnumbered, inadequately armed, and too tired to put up any real resistance. Most of Turner's men were killed. The rest were captured, except the Prophet himself and four of his companions. By the end of the day Turner was alone.

He made it into the deep woods, where he waited, hoping some of his men would rally and resume their rebellion. Rewards totaling $1,100 were offered for his capture, and at least 500 whites spent days scouring the woods for him.

No cry for mercy penetrated their flinty bosoms. Never did a band of savages do their work of death more unsparingly.

Thomas R. Gray, The Confessions of Nat Turner (1831)

People reported seeing him as far away as Baltimore and the free state of Ohio, but in fact he never left Southampton County. "On Thursday night," as he recounted in his confession, "after having supplied myself with provisions from Mr. Travis's, I scratched a hole under a pile of fence rails in a field, where I concealed myself for six weeks, never leaving my hiding place but for a few

minutes in the dead of night to get water." Discovered by two slaves, he begged for help, but when they fled he no longer had any hope. "Knowing then they would betray me," he reported sadly, "I immediately left my hiding place and was pursued almost incessantly until I was taken a fortnight afterwards." On October 30th Nat Turner was discovered crouching in a new hole he had dug for himself with his sword, about a mile and a half from the Travis farm.

Turner was tried within days. He denied nothing and offered no defense, but accepted his fate and the full responsibility for the uprising. Yet he pleaded "Not Guilty," explaining to his lawyer that he did not feel guilty for what he had done. During the trial he announced that if he had another chance he would take the same bloody path to God again. "Indiscriminate slaughter was not their intention after they obtained a foothold," Turner was reported as declaring of himself and his fellow rebels, "and was resorted to in the first instance to strike terror and alarm. Women and children would afterward have been spared and men too who ceased to resist." The court was not moved by this declaration, and Turner was sentenced as emphatically as Denmark Vesey had been. "You have been arraigned and tried before this court, and convicted of one of the highest crimes in the criminal code," the judge intoned.

> You have been convicted of plotting in cold blood, the indiscriminate destruction of men, of helpless women, and of infant children. The evidence before us leaves not a shadow of doubt, but that your hands were often imbrued in the blood of the innocent. . . . The judgment of the court is that you be taken hence to the jail from whence you came, thence to the place of execution, and . . . be hung by the neck until you are dead! dead! dead! and may the Lord have mercy on your soul.

Turner accepted the sentence with silent dignity, as he did his execution. Fifty-three slaves had been arrested in connec-

# Benjamin Banneker _____

African Americans fought against slavery in many ways, some by armed resistance and some by their lives and their work. One of the most remarkable soldiers in the war for justice was a quiet, studious man who spent his whole life alone on a small tobacco farm calculating figures and studying the stars.

Benjamin Banneker was born in 1731 in Maryland. The son of a freed slave, he had little formal education, but his scientific accomplishments provided opponents of slavery with an important argument against the belief in African inferiority.

At the age of 21 he built a wooden clock that kept perfect time for over 50 years. Although he had never seen such a clock before, he carved every wheel and gear by hand with a jackknife. Later, with books borrowed from a Quaker neighbor, he studied mathematics and astronomy and became so proficient a surveyor that he was hired to help lay out the new capital city of Washington, D.C. When he was 60 years old, he

tion with the uprising, and a total of 20 were hanged. Turner died last of all, on November 11th. According to oral tradition, the crowd gathered around the gallows saw a sign in the heavens on that day. "The sun was hidden behind angry clouds, the thunder rolled, the lightning flashed," reported one witness, "and the most terrific storm visited that county ever known."

While waiting for execution, Turner made a confession to Thomas R. Gray, one of the lawyers appointed to represent him. Gray was a white slave owner and far from sympathetic to his client, but he could not help being impressed by him. "For natural intelligence and quickness of apprehension," he wrote, "[Turner] is surpassed by few men I have ever seen." Gray was also a little frightened by Turner. "The calm, deliberate composure with which he spoke of his late deeds and intentions, the expression of taught himself trigonometry and calculus and began to publish a series of astronomical almanacs, predicting the weather and calculating the tides. Antislavery activists used his work to prove, as one wrote in the first volume of his almanac in 1791, that "the powers of the mind are disconnected with the colour of the skin."

Banneker did not become involved in any organized rebellion against slavery, but he felt deeply about its injustice. In 1791 he sent a copy of his almanac to Thomas Jefferson, then secretary of state, with a letter reminding him of his own words, in the Declaration of Independence, stating that "all men are created equal." One of the most eloquent protests against slavery written by an African American, Banneker's letter challenged the statesman to support the cause of racial equality instead of "detaining by fraud and violence so numerous a part of my brethren under groaning captivity and cruel oppression."

Banneker lived to the age of 75, working alone on his mathematical calculations. His almanacs, which appeared in some 30 editions during his lifetime, are no longer used, but his achievements stand as an early monument to the intellectual capacities of African Americans.◆

his fiend-like face when excited by enthusiasm, still bearing the blood of helpless innocence about him," he wrote in his report of Turner's confession, "clothed with rags and covered with chains; yet daring to raise his manacled hands to heaven, with a spirit soaring above the attributes of man; I looked on him and my blood curdled in my veins."

Turner has been depicted, in his own time and later, as both a madman and a hero, a monster and a martyr. But that he was carrying out God's plan and doing His work, Turner himself never doubted. As he sat in his prison cell, he described to Gray one of the heavenly signs he had received. The lawyer, seeing him in chains and about to be hanged for murder, could not resist interrupting to ask, "Do you not find yourself mistaken now?" Nat Turner replied without hesitation, "Was not Christ crucified?"

## The Results of the Nat Turner Revolt

The revolt in Southampton County was brief, and relatively few people were directly involved. Its real significance lay in the consequences it had for slavery in America.

The South had lived with great tension over the slavery question for many years. Fear of rebellion had become hysterical throughout the slave states, and antislavery propaganda from the North reinforced this fear. After every uprising, the laws governing slaves became stricter. During the Nat Turner uprising, slaves for the first time had actually carried out their plans to murder whites, and had done so with all the ferocity their masters had feared. After Nat Turner's revolt, fear turned to panic, and a bloodbath followed. The military began it. As one modern scholar explains it, the army troops and militiamen arrived in Southampton County "burning with wrath" and, finding no insurgents to shoot, they began to shoot any African American they saw.

Determined to teach slaves a lesson, whites far outdid Nat Turner's men in violence. Even the Southern press, usually supportive of the slave-owning class, was horrified. One North Carolina newspaperman reported, "All day long, the slaughter kept up from time to time as they fell in with the Negroes, one hundred and twenty being killed in one day." Civilians set up their own vigilante groups, terrorizing slaves and free African Americans alike.

> The Massacre of the whites has ceased and the destruction of the Negroes has started.
>
>
>
> The Washington Globe,
> August 29, 1831

A former slave, recalling those days, described the patrols that harassed African Americans, looking for any excuse to punish them. "Colored people and slaves who lived in remote parts of the town suffered in an especial manner," she wrote. "In some cases the searchers scattered powder and shot among their clothes, and then sent other parties to find them, and bring them forward as proof that they were plotting insurrection. Every where men, women, and children were whipped till the blood stood in puddles at their feet."

The prisons overflowed with suspects, and the courts tried, convicted, and executed suspects in record time. African Americans were struck down by roving gangs of whites, and bodies lay strewn along the main road. The head of one slave was stuck on a post at an intersection, to serve as a warning. The number murdered in this frenzy of retribution can never be known, and the massacre ended only when the county government refused to compensate owners for slaves killed by mob action.

In this atmosphere of panic, no group was safe from attack. Nat Turner had known how to read and write, so laws against teaching slaves were strengthened. Turner had preached, so religious freedom was curtailed, and Virginia passed a law stating that "no slave, free negro, or mulatto, whether he shall have been ordained or licensed, or otherwise, shall hereafter undertake to preach, exhort, or conduct, or hold any assembly or meeting, for religious or other purposes, either in the day time or at night." Free African Americans, always a dangerous class in the eyes of Southern whites, were especially singled out as a threat, and they were banished by law from many regions. Whites looked under their beds every night and slept with weapons under their pillows. The South became an armed camp.

The rebellion had a psychological effect on slaves, too. If at first it was inspiring as evidence that slaves could act together and carry out a strike for freedom, its awful results were proof of the impossible odds against success in such an enterprise. The rebellion collapsed in days, received little support from slaves, and was followed by weeks of horrible reprisals against African Americans in every slave state. Whatever feeble antislavery sentiment had existed in the South disappeared in the face of the violent sentiment that spread against it. Turner was a hero and martyr to many slaves and to people sympathetic to them, but everyone had to recognize that his rebellion had only tightened the chains that bound them. There was never a major slave uprising after Turner's.

## NOTES

p. 91 "I saw white spirits . . ." Thomas R. Gray, *The Confessions of Nat Turner* (1831; reprinted in John Kendrik Clarke, ed., *William Styron's Nat Turner: Ten Black Writers Respond* (1968; Westport, Conn.: Greenwood Press, 1987), p. 102.

p. 93 "I entered my master's chamber . . ." Gray, p. 105.

p. 94 "On Thursday night . . ." Gray, p. 111.

p. 95 "Indiscriminate slaughter was not their intention . . ." Richmond, Virginia *Inquirer*, November 8, 1831.

p. 95 "You have been arraigned . . ." Gray, p. 116.

p. 96 "The sun was hidden . . ." George W. Williams, *History of the Negro Race in America, 1619–1880* (1883; New York: Arno Press, 1968), vol. II, p. 90.

p. 96 "For natural intelligence . . ." Gray, p. 113.

p. 97 "Do you not find yourself mistaken now?" Gray, p. 104

p. 98 "All day long, the slaughter kept up . . ." *The North Carolina Star*, September 13, 1831.

p. 98–99 "Colored people and slaves . . ." Harriet A. Jacobs, *Incidents in the Life of a Slave Girl* (1861; quoted in William Dudley, ed., *Slavery: Opposing Viewpoints* (San Diego, Calif.: Greenhaven Press, 1992), p. 146.

p. 99 "no slave, free negro, or mulatto . . ." Quoted in Herbert Aptheker, *Negro Slave Revolts in The United States* (1943; New York: International Publishers, 1993), p. 314.

# 8

# Slave Mutinies: Rebellion on the High Seas

$N$at Turner's uprising turned out to be the last important one in the American South because white society proved, with its brutal response, that such efforts were hopeless. The power of an armed militia, supported by the military force of the national government, was too great for isolated bands of rebels to combat. But on board a slave ship, the situation was somewhat different. Though mariners protected themselves with chains and whips from those they transported, slaves almost always outnumbered the crews of the vessels that carried them. Ship captains in the Middle Passage, or carrying slaves between markets in the New World, feared mutinies most of all. In the first century of the trade, British slavers averaged one mutiny every two years, and the French experienced one mutiny in every 15 voyages, averaging one every year and a half. Most cost the slave owners money; all cost slaves their lives. Few were successful.

But as the failed rebellions of Gabriel, Vesey, and Turner, and the successful one in Saint-Domingue, inspired increasing sympathy for slaves among previously indifferent people in the United States, public feeling about such uprisings began to change. Haiti and Jamaica, in both of which slavery had been abolished in 1804, viewed African rebels as heroes, and any that could escape to those free islands would be assured of a welcome. Antislavery organizations in the northern American states actively supported fugitives and rebels, both in their writings and with practical help. Whenever possible, Northern opponents of slavery challenged the system in the federal courts by defending slaves. Since the U.S. Constitution essentially supported the rights of slave owners, slaves seldom won their cases in court. But times were changing, and sometimes there were surprises. No surprise was more disturbing to the South than the courtroom drama of the schooner *Amistad*. Although the *Amistad* case did not concern American slaves or slave owners directly, it rocked Southern slavery to its foundations.

## Cinqué and the Amistad

The story begins in Havana, Cuba, in the summer of 1839, when two Spaniards made an investment at the public slave market. José Ruiz, a shrewd young businessman of 24, bought 49 able-bodied African men for $450 apiece, and his older companion Pedro Montes, 58, made the more modest purchase of three little girls and one small boy, all under 12 years old. Slavery was still legal in Cuba (which did not abolish it until 1886), but the importation of new slaves onto the island had been abolished in 1820. Since all 53 slaves had been recently brought in from Africa, they were technically contraband, but there was no danger from the Cuban authorities—the laws regarding the importation of slaves were regularly ignored there. Nevertheless, if the dealers were caught in Caribbean waters by English authorities, their cargo could be seized and released. So Ruiz and Montes were cautious with their valuable property, which they intended to sell in Puerto Príncipe, Cuba, a few days' sail from Havana.

Ruiz and Montes hired the schooner *Amistad*, a sleek black ship built in Baltimore for the slave trade, and on the hot night of June 28 they loaded it. They herded their slaves into the hold, chained together and with iron collars locked around their necks. Each slave, including the four children, was provided with a false Spanish passport, although all spoke only native African languages and would never have passed for Spanish if they had been challenged. At midnight, the slaver set sail for Guanaja, the port of entry for Puerto Príncipe, some 300 miles away. They never arrived.

Conditions on the boat, whose name means "friendship" in Spanish, were not very friendly. The owner and captain, Ramon Ferrer, was in a hurry and decided not to make any stops along the way for provisions. The slaves were each allotted one banana, two potatoes, and half a cup of water per day. When one of them tried to get more water, Ruiz ordered him flogged.

Unable to communicate with their captors, the slaves were completely helpless. One of them made signs to the cook, a free mulatto named Celestino, asking what was to become of them. Celestino evidently enjoyed his power over the slaves; he grinned and replied with gestures that their heads

The Amistad *mutiny was perhaps the most publicized of all maritime slave revolts.* This *imaginative depiction of it appeared in many publications at the time.* (Library of Congress)

were to be cut off, and they were then to be chopped up, salted, and eaten by the crew. It was not an encouraging beginning for the voyage.

## The Mutiny

The young African who had asked the question, a powerfully built 25-year-old named Joseph Cinqué (Pronounced Sin-kay), determined not to die without a fight. He found a nail in the hold and quietly flattened it to pick the lock of his iron collar. All but three of the slaves were from Mende, on the west coast of Africa in Sierra Leone, and they spoke the same language. The crew spoke only Spanish, so the slaves were able to discuss their situation openly and develop a plan for escape. They agreed to make a bid for freedom at the first opportunity.

The third night out, July first, was a stormy one. Cinqué waited until the captain and crew had gone to sleep and released himself and the others around 4:00 A.M. They had noticed that the cargo included a load of knives with blades 2 feet long, made for cutting sugarcane. The slaves noise-lessly armed themselves with these and climbed to the deck.

In minutes they killed the captain and hacked the mulatto cook to pieces. The rest of the crew consisted of two sailors, who disappeared in the confusion and probably drowned trying swim the 20 miles to shore. The captain's cabin boy, a 16-year-old slave named Antonio, begged for his life, and the mutineers spared him. The only whites remaining were the slaves' two former owners, Ruiz and Montes, both wounded and now slaves themselves. Cinqué was master of the vessel.

None of the slaves knew anything about running a ship, and so they agreed to leave Ruiz and Montes alive to steer them back to Africa. Montes had been a sea captain. He was put at the helm, under Cinqué's orders, and told to head into the rising sun—the direction the slaves remembered coming from when they were taken from their homes.

Montes did nothing of the sort. Knowing that the mutineers did not understand navigation, he kept the schooner moving slowly eastward by day and then changed course every night, steering north and west toward the United States. For weeks Montes led them back and forth through the Caribbean waters, hoping to be picked up and freed by Americans or Cubans. In fact, several merchant vessels did see the *Amistad*, but they were so frightened at the sight of black men with long knives on the deck that they steered away from the ship, thinking the men were pirates.

The little food on board soon disappeared, and some of the mutineers were so thirsty that they drank the bottles of medicine in storage, poisoning themselves. In all, 10 of the Africans died during this dreadful voyage. Cinqué finally realized that he had no choice but to put ashore for provisions. One day he ordered the schooner to land at the next island they saw. He had no idea where they were.

In fact, after 63 days of zigzagging, they had reached New York's Long Island. The vessel was seized and the mutineers promptly arrested for piracy and murder. Ruiz and Montes were set free, asserting that the *Amistad* was a Spanish slave ship legally transporting slaves from one place to another in Cuba. They demanded that their property—including the slaves—be restored to them. Because New York was a free state, Lieutenant Gedney, who had seized the schooner, had it towed to Connecticut, where slavery was still legal. There, he thought, he might claim the slaveship and its cargo as salvage. The *Amistad* was in bad shape, but the 43 surviving Africans would be a valuable prize.

## The Trial

The arrival of the slaves in New London, Connecticut caused a sensation. All the Africans, including the four children and Antonio, the cabin boy, were put in the New Haven jail while the court tried to sort out what to do with them and with the *Amistad*. It was a knotty problem involving marine law, international law, questions of local and national jurisdiction, and property rights. Lieutenant Gedney brought a lawsuit claiming the boat, its cargo, and all the slaves as salvage. Because Cuba was a possession of Spain, the Spanish government demanded that the slaves be returned to Havana to be tried for piracy and murder. Ruiz, who had paid more than $22,000 for his slaves, wanted either them or his money back. The American president, Martin Van Buren, wanted good diplomatic relations with Spain and urged sending the slaves back to Havana. To confuse matters further, no one could get the Africans' side of the story or even figure out what language they spoke.

In time, a professor of linguistics at Yale not only discovered what the slaves' language was but found a Mende sailor in New York to act as their interpreter. The account of their illegal enslavement and their daring mutiny, as reported by the Mende James Covey, became the story of the year throughout the country. The most active opponents of slavery, who called themselves abolitionists, saw the case as an ideal opportunity to bring their cause to the conscience of the American people. Within a week they had organized an *Amistad* Committee to defend the slaves in court.

The Southern states vigorously opposed freeing the slaves, recognizing a threat to the institution on which their economy was still based. In the North, feelings ran high in favor of the slaves. The handsome and magnetic Cinqué became a hero in the Northern press. Although there was and is no evidence that he had held a high station in Africa, the newspapers elevated him to royalty. The noted poet William Cullen Bryant wrote a poem calling him The African Chief:

> Chained in a foreign land he stood,
> A man of giant frame,
> Amid the gathering multitude
> That shrank to hear his name—
>
> . . . . . . . . . . . .
>
> The scars his dark broad bosom wore
> Showed warrior true and brave;
> A prince among his tribe before,
> He *could not be a slave.*

Abolitionists rallied from several states. Lewis and Arthur Tappan, wealthy New York merchants and descendants of Benjamin Franklin, gathered funds to support the slaves. Roger Sherman Baldwin, grandson of one of the signers of the Declaration of Independence and a prominent constitutional layer in New Haven, undertook their defense. He based his case on the fact that the importation of slaves into Cuba was illegal and the *Amistad* group had arrived in Havana after the law prohibiting the importation of slaves went into effect. Antonio, the cabin boy, testified that the slaves had been brought to Cuba just months before, and of course the children were too young to have been born in Cuba before 1820. Therefore, Baldwin argued, Cinqué and the others were not legally slaves, and their mutiny was justified by "the inherant right of self defense."

The courtroom was packed. People came from around the country, and Yale Law School closed during the trial so that its students could attend. The lawyers on both sides argued their cases fervently. According to one observer, Cinqué delivered a speech in his native Mende so dramatically that it moved the jury even before Covey translated it.

The trial lasted all winter, but at last the Federal District Court of Connecticut found in favor of the slaves and directed that they be freed. Only Antonio was ordered returned, as he was the "legal slave" of Captain Ferrer. This made an important point, because it established that the court had not declared slavery illegal; it acquitted the mutineers only because they were *not* slaves. As one modern scholar has noted, the Van Buren administration, which supported slavery, had lost the case in Connecticut, but it had won a victory by establishing in court that slaves from foreign countries would not be freed if they came to the United States. The question didn't matter in the case of Antonio. Because he was not charged with participation in the mutiny, he was not held in prison. When the authorities came to send him back to Cuba, he had disappeared. He had simply left Connecticut and gone to Canada, where he had found a job. In Canada he was a free man.

The Spanish government would not let the matter rest. It was a point of international law that the rights of property be respected. And since the American government wanted to stay on good terms with Spain, it directed the U.S. district attorney to appeal the decision of the federal court. A higher court heard the case, and supported the decision of the Connecticut court, once again declaring the rebels free. And once

*The public vengeance has not been satisfied, for be it recollected that the Legation of Spain does not demand the delivery of slaves but of assassins.*

Spanish Ambassador
Pedro Alcántara de Argaiz, note to
U.S. Secretary of State
John Forsyth, September 6, 1839

again the case was appealed. For months lawyers and politicians argued their way through a tangle of claims and counterclaims from court to court, with the U.S. Justice Department insisting on returning the prisoners to Spain and the courts continuing to deny the appeals. In 1841, the case reached the end of the line—the Supreme Court.

By now the *Amistad* case had became a major national issue. Many people who until then had remained more or less indifferent began to question whether the country had the right to send free men into foreign slavery. The appearance of the case before the highest court in the land was clearly a turning point in American history. In Washington, the abolitionists approached John Quincy Adams to defend the case.

Adams was the eldest son of John Adams, the second president of the United States; he had served as secretary of state under James Monroe and as the sixth president, and now, in his seventies, he was a member of the House of Representatives from Massachusetts. For years he had been introducing bills against slavery in the House. He had not appeared in court as a practicing lawyer for over 30 years, but his skill in the courtroom was still formidable.

The prisoners did not know his reputation; to them he was just another lawyer involved in their bewildering and seemingly endless trial. During all this time, they had been kept in detention in Connecticut. Though the children had been placed in sympathetic homes, and all the prisoners were being well treated and were receiving lessons in English and religion, they were understandably getting impatient. Their continued captivity was as frustrating to them as their imprisonment on the *Amistad* had been. One of them, Kale, wrote to Adams, "We want you to ask the Court what we have done wrong. What for Americans keep us in prison. Some people say Mendi people crazy; Mendi people dolt, because we no talk American language. Merica people no talk Mendi language; Merica people dolt?"

# The American Colonization Society ___

Slaves who mutinied on board ships had one goal: to return to their native continent. Many whites, including Abraham Lincoln, also thought the return of all blacks to Africa would be the best solution to the race problem in the United States. As early as 1800, Thomas Jefferson had favored the gradual end of slavery and the mass deportation of everyone of African descent, however long they or their families had been in America. In this way, he felt, the country could prevent what he considered the dangerous mixing of the races.

In the South, the idea of returning free blacks to Africa was appealing. Old or sick slaves who were no longer able to work could be released and would not have to be supported. Even more important to slave owners, deportation of free African Americans would get rid of people whose agitation encouraged slaves to rebel. In the North, the competition of free black laborers with the new immigrant population for jobs would be eliminated. Shipping all free African Americans off to Africa would solve several problems at once.

In 1817, the American Society for Colonizing the Free People of Color of the United States was formed. It persuaded Congress to buy land in West Africa and establish the colony of Monrovia, later renamed Liberia (from the Latin word for "free"). The plan was to settle all free Ameri-

Adams was moved, and he determined to show that "Merica people" were *not* dolt, and were not unjust, either. On March 9, 1841, he spoke in defense of the Africans, drawing on all his passionate spirit and formidable intelligence. He argued not only that the slave trade was illegal in both Spanish and American law, but that all mankind had a natural right to freedom. "Old Man Eloquent," as he was called, spoke for eight and a half hours that day. Although a majority of the justices came from the South, his speech was so persuasive that they rose above their state loyalties and ordered the mutineers released.

can blacks, and all Africans liberated from slave ships, in a country of their own.

At first the idea was popular among both slave owners and people who wanted to end slavery. But there were several arguments against colonization. First, it would be impossibly expensive to end slavery, since to buy and transport all the slaves in the United States would cost an estimated $1.5 trillion. Second, free African Americans vigorously opposed the idea of resettlement, recognizing it as essentially a racist plot to prevent blacks from entering American society. "Why should we leave this land so dearly bought by the blood, groans and tears of our fathers?" demanded one African-American group. "This is our home; here let us live and here let us die."

The American Colonization Society, as it was popularly called, was not a success. By 1852, fewer than 8,000 people had been sent to Liberia—about 2,800 free African Americans, 3,600 released from slavery on condition that they leave the country, and 1,000 liberated from slave ships. In the 60 years that followed before the Society was officially disbanded in 1912, the total grew by a scant 4,000.

Although the colonization experiment failed to solve America's racial problems, the country it brought into being still survives as an independent nation, and the descendants of some of the slaves who settled it have prospered there. The first self-governing republic in Africa, Liberia was one of the founders of the United Nations and now supports a population of almost three million.◆

The Spanish government had no further legal recourse, but was determined to pursue the case anyway. It demanded repayment for the value of its citizens' ship and slaves. Van Buren, still trying to maintain friendly relations with Spain and himself deeply opposed to abolitionism, urged that the country pay the claim. Congress did not agree to do so, and the case dragged on for years. As late as 1858, President James Buchanan recommended that the heirs of Captain Ferrer, the owner of the *Amistad*, be reimbursed, and still Congress refused. Spain never got a penny.

For Cinqué and his friends, the case was closed in 1841. Following the Supreme Court decision, some of them went on a speaking tour to raise money for their trip back to Africa. According to a contemporary account, Cinqué spoke Mende "in a very graceful and animated manner." Kale, the one who had written to Adams, spoke in English, and the three girls read passages from the Bible. By November, they had collected enough for the long journey. Of the 53 who had shared the fateful last voyage of the slaver *Amistad*, 35 remained. They returned to Africa, accompanied by James Covey, who had decided to return to his native home.

Cinqué and his friends arrived in Africa in January 1842, nearly three years after they had made the journey in chains on the Middle Passage. The boat docked in Sierra Leone, and most of the group continued the journey to their native Mende. Cinqué returned to his wife and three children, but he remained in touch with the organization that had freed him. The *Amistad* Committee joined other groups to form the American Missionary Association in 1846, and later Cinqué worked for their mission at Kaw-Mende as an interpreter. He died around 1879.

## *The* Creole

The *Amistad* case gave abolitionists their first real opportunity to promote the abolition of slavery, and the commanding appearance and manner of Cinqué provided the movement with its first romantic hero. Shortly after the case was decided, another mutiny brought the issue to the fore again. This time the shoe was on the other foot.

On October 15, 1841, an American brigantine named the *Creole* left Virginia for Louisiana, transporting more than 130 slaves belonging to a man named McCargo. Like the *Amistad*, it never reached its destination. On November 7, three weeks into the voyage, McCargo's human cargo rebelled, killing one man and wounding the captain. Under the leadership of a powerful African American with the resounding name of Madison Washington, 19 of the slaves swiftly overcame the crew and gave them the choice of steering the two-masted ship to an English port or being thrown overboard. The slaves knew that Great Britain had abolished slavery in all its colonies in 1807, and hoped for the same asylum the United States had so reluctantly given the *Amistad* slaves six months before.

*Portrait of Joseph Cinqué, painted from life by Nathaniel Jocelyn.* (New York Public Library, Schomburg Center for Research in Black Culture)

> The claims of the slave dealers are preposterous for slaves in England are free: the chains of bondage fall from their limbs, once their feet have pressed English soil.
>
>
>
> *Liberator*, February 11, 1842

The organizers of the *Creole* mutiny were luckier than Cinqué and his friends had been; the crew obeyed their orders and landed at the British port of Nassau in the Bahamas, where they were warmly welcomed by boatloads of free Africans who rowed out to greet them. Now it was America's turn to call for the return of slaves, both as valuable property and as criminals to be punished for mutiny and murder. The American consul in Nassau demanded the arrest of the slaves, just as the Spanish ambassador had in the *Amistad* case. And of course the unlucky Mr. McCargo wanted his property back.

The abolitionists were happy to find another case to help publicize their cause. They protested vigorously that because British law did not recognize slavery, any slave who reached a British colony was automatically free. The populace of Nassau felt the same way: There were huge public demonstrations calling for the Africans' release. The British authorities didn't even bother with a court trial—they simply released the American slaves. Despite repeated American protests, and even threats of war, the British also refused to extradite Washington and the other mutineers.

The tide was turning. Slave rebellions were not only gaining some popular sympathy and support, they were sometimes actually succeeding.

**NOTES**

p. 107  "Chained in a foreign land . . ." William Cullen Bryant, in the abolitionist magazine *Emancipator*, September 19, 1839.

p. 109  "We want you to ask the Court . . ." Kale, letter to John Quincy Adams, printed in the *Emancipator*, March 12, 1841.

# 9

# How It Ended: What Slave Resistance Accomplished

T he success of the revo-
lution in Haiti and of the *Amistad* and *Creole* mutinies
proved deeply satisfying to American slaves and their sym-
pathizers, but they provided no solution to the problem at
home. Successful armed rebellion in the American South
remained virtually impossible. Of the many recorded uprisings, large and small, none succeeded, and all resulted in
worse conditions and greater repression for slaves. Gabriel,

THE

AMERICAN

ANTI-SLAVERY

ALMANAC,

FOR

1839,

BEING THE THIRD AFTER BISSEXTILE OR LEAP-YEAR, AND THE
63D OF AMERICAN INDEPENDENCE. CALCULATED FOR
BOSTON ; ADAPTED TO THE NEW ENGLAND STATES.

What has the North to do with Slavery ?

" Have no *fellowship* with the unfruitful works of darkness, but rather *reprove* them. "

NEW YORK & BOSTON:

PUBLISHED FOR THE AMERICAN ANTI-SLAVERY SOCIETY.

NEW YORK : — S. W. BENEDICT, 143, NASSAU ST.

BOSTON : — ISAAC KNAPP, 25, CORNHILL.

*One of the objectives of the abolitionist movement in the North was to lend
support to fugitive slaves.* (New York Public Library Picture Collection)

Denmark Vesey, and Nat Turner failed to improve the condition of their people, and individual acts—the confrontations, sabotage, and escape of slaves over a period of three centuries—did nothing directly to alter the system they defied.

Nevertheless, it was the efforts of the slaves themselves that brought slavery down after all. Every bid for an end to their oppression, successful or unsuccessful, sustained the slaves' quest for freedom. And every rebellion, every gesture of defiance, every flight weakened the authority of the whites who held them captive.

## Abolitionism

Resistance demonstrated that slaves' possessed both the desire and the capacity for the independence that their masters denied them. The army of people willing to fight against slavery grew every year. Organizations calling for abolition had existed as early as the 17th century. The Religious Society of Friends, commonly called Quakers, were powerfully influenced by slave rebellion. Quakers, a Christian sect deeply concerned with social reform, supported pacifism, improvement of prison conditions, and women's rights, but their most important program was the fight against slavery. They found proof that slaves were discontented, as well as evidence of African intelligence and determination, in the stories of slave rebellions. Pennsylvania Quakers founded the first American antislavery organization in the 1700s and frequently petitioned the government to end the slave trade. When Gabriel's conspiracy panicked the South, they were the only group in that region that continued to speak out for abolition.

The Quakers were pioneers in the struggle for racial equality, but formal protest against slavery was not exclusively a white religious crusade. Former slaves were outspo-

> *As miserable, wretched, degraded and abject as you have made us . . . to support you and your families . . . some of you (whites) on the continent of America, will yet curse the day that you were ever born. . . . My colour will yet root some of you out of the very face of the earth!!!!!!*
>
>
>
> David Walker, *Appeal* (1829)

ken opponents of the institution, and many became active abolitionists. In 1817, a large group of free African Americans formed the Convention of Color to speak for their enslaved brothers. When their respectful petitions failed to move legislators, their pleas became demands.

## David Walker

In 1829, a free African American named David Walker published a pamphlet that differed from the usual antislavery tract. Born in North Carolina in 1785, Walker remembered the turmoil created by Gabriel and Vesey, and he warned the country of what was to come if slavery persisted. In words that echoed in the writings of black militants a century and a half later, he challenged the white community:

> Remember, Americans, that we must and shall be free, and enlightened as you are, will you wait until we shall, under God obtain our liberty by the crushing arm of power? Will it not be dreadful for you? . . . We must and shall be free, I say, in spite of you. You may do your best to keep us in wretchedness and misery, to enrich you and your children, but God will deliver us from under you. And wo, wo will be to you if we have to obtain our freedom by fighting.

Published in Boston at his own expense, Walker's *Appeal* was a bombshell in the South, where it was interpreted less as an appeal than as a threat. Circulating it was declared a criminal offense in many states, yet it quickly ran through three editions and found its way into the hands of slaves throughout the South. Some historians believe that Nat Turner read it and was influenced by it. The *Appeal* so alarmed a group in Georgia that they offered $10,000 to anyone who could deliver Walker alive, or $1,000 for his body. In 1830, a year after the *Appeal's* publication, Walker was found dead in a doorway near his home in Boston. No one ever claimed the reward, but many believed he was murdered. Today he is considered the father of black nationalism.

## William Lloyd Garrison

Antislavery activists in the North were electrified by Walker's powerful words, though many were alarmed by his angry tone. The Quaker abolitionist Benjamin Lundy, the leading voice of the movement at the time, believed in gradual emancipation, reimbursement for slave owners, and possibly relocation of ex-slaves back to Africa. Lundy found the *Appeal* dangerously inflammatory, but many others found it convincing. In 1831, Lundy's disciple and colleague William Lloyd Garrison revised his moderate position and called for an immediate, unqualified end to slavery. In that year the 34-year-old Garrison began publication in Boston of his weekly magazine *Liberator* with the ringing words: "I shall contend for the immediate enfranchisement of our slave population—I will be as harsh as truth and as uncompromising as justice on this subject—I do not wish to think, or speak, or write with moderation— . . . I will not retreat a single inch, *and I will be heard*!"

And heard he was. Garrison became the most effective white advocate of freedom and full citizenship for African Americans. A fervent crusader, he was far more extreme than

Lundy. He opposed repayment of slave owners, and he recognized the racist motives for the movement to "colonize" ex-slaves by deporting them. Because the Constitution did not forbid slavery, he denounced it on the front page of his magazine as "a covenant with death and an agreement with Hell" and once publicly burned a copy in the streets of Boston, shouting "So perish all compromises with tyranny!" In 1833, he formed the American Anti-Slavery Society, a radical reform organization. The first American political group open to members of both races and to women, it was highly controversial, and its meetings were often broken up by angry mobs.

Garrison's tirades won him a reputation as a fanatic, not only among supporters of slavery but even among more conservative abolitionists. Though he never openly called for rebellion, many people considered the Nat Turner uprising, occurring just eight months after the first issue of the *Liberator*, to be a result of his deliberate provocation. Southern legislators demanded the magazine's suppression and called for Garrison's arrest for inciting slaves to revolt. But the *Liberator* continued to appear for more than 30 years and ceased publication only when Garrison felt it had finished its work, with the end of slavery in 1865.

*William Lloyd Garrison was a leading abolitionist writer and speaker.* (New York Public Library Picture Collection)

## Henry Highland Garnet

Such firebrands as Walker and Garrison demanded reform without advocating violence. In 1843, however, a voice was raised calling for stronger measures. Henry Highland Garnet spoke to a Convention of Color meeting in Buffalo, New York, delivering an address that was a true call to arms.

Garnet had been born a slave in Maryland in 1815. At the age of nine he escaped with his family to New York, where he grew up to become a Presbyterian minister. A dynamic speaker, he issued the boldest attack on slavery yet made by an African American. Reminding his listeners at the convention of the "martyr to freedom" Denmark Vesey, "the patriotic" Nathaniel Turner (numbered "among the noble and brave"), "the immortal Joseph Cinqué, the hero of the *Amistad*," and "that bright star of freedom" Madison Washington, he called on his audience to follow the heroic example of these rebels:

> In the name of the Merciful God! and by all that life is worth, let it no longer be a debatable question, whether it is better to choose LIBERTY or DEATH. . . . From this moment cease to labor for tyrants. . . . Let every slave throughout the land do this, and the days of slavery are numbered. You cannot be more oppressed than you have been—you cannot suffer greater cruelties than you have already. RATHER DIE FREEMEN THAN LIVE TO BE SLAVES.

Garnet concluded his oration with this challenge:

> In the name of God we ask, are you men? Where is the blood of your fathers? Has it all run out of your veins? Awake, awake. . . . Heaven as with a voice of thunder calls on you to arise from the dust. Let your motto be RESISTANCE! RESISTANCE! RESISTANCE!

# Uncle Tom's Cabin

The tracts of the abolitionists argued with great moral fervor for the end of slavery and described the cruelty of the institution movingly, but no book had as great an impact on public thought as Harriet Beecher Stowe's novel Uncle Tom's Cabin. First serialized in an antislavery newspaper in 1851–52, it was then published in book form, selling 10,000 copies in less than a week and more than 300,000 in its first six months. Hated in the South, it became an international best-seller, being translated into 37 languages. In Scotland, it led to the formation of an "emancipation fund," and it would contribute to the end of slavery in countries as far away as Russia and Siam.

Mrs. Stowe's moving story, subtitled Life Among the Lowly, was the first novel to have an African-American hero. The daughter of a noted clergyman, Mrs. Stowe grew up in Connecticut. She had little firsthand contact with slavery but often heard her father denounce it from the

Garnet asked the convention to adopt his speech as its official statement, and they came very close to doing so. But because "the document was war-like, and encouraged insurrection," thus endangering the lives of members living near the borders of slave states, they voted it down after much debate. Still, the white community got the idea. These "colored conventions" gave the country a clear idea of how African Americans felt, and of their growing impatience for freedom.

## The Underground Railroad

The bold speech of abolitionists often put them at great risk. Some outspoken advocates of African-American freedom, like Walker, paid for their courage with their lives; and many, pulpit. When Congress passed the cruel Fugitive Slave Law of 1850, she was so horrified that she determined to write a novel exposing slavery. "I feel as if I had written some of it almost with my heart's blood," she later reported.

*Uncle Tom's Cabin* focuses on the life and tragic death of Uncle Tom, a pious slave sold by a Kentucky family because they have lost their money. In time he falls into the hands of the vicious, drunken planter Simon Legree, who flogs him to death because he refuses to recognize anyone but God as his master. Although "Uncle Tom" has become a synonym for a passive, obedient African American, the character was intended by Stowe as a sympathetic portrait—Uncle Tom is presented as a model of Christian patience who defies his master and dies for his principles.

The long novel contains dramatic details of the Underground Railroad, is full of vividly portrayed characters, and has a plot rich with incidents both humorous and pathetic. So effectively did it stir Northern feeling against slavery that when Lincoln met the author during the Civil War, he is reported to have exclaimed, "So you're the little woman who wrote the book that made this great war!"◆

including Garrison, spent time in jail. But there were those who did more than write and speak against slavery. Some gave active support to slaves. As early as the 1780s, George Washington complained of the Quakers' helping slaves to freedom, and by the 1830s a network of organized support emerged. Called the Underground Railroad, it had no tracks or cars and charged no fares, but was rather a loose system of help for fugitives. It was composed mostly of free Northern African Americans, called "conductors," who met escaped slaves at fixed "stations," hid them if necessary until the search parties gave up looking, and then guided them to safety further north. White abolitionist societies participated in the work and helped the fugitives at the end of the line. These organizations welcomed such escaped slaves as the Crafts and Box Brown (whose stories are told in chapter 3 of this book) when they reached Pennsylvania.

Free and Slave Areas, United States, 1860
(with dates of emancipation)

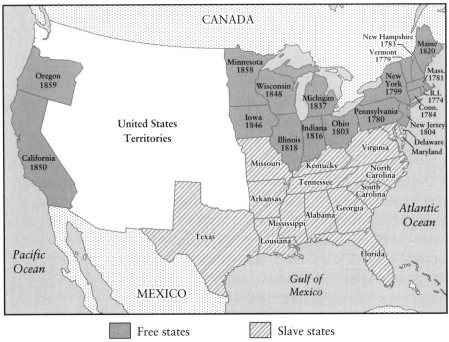

Free states    Slave states

One of the most active conductors on the Underground Railroad was William Still, the secretary of the Pennsylvania Society for the Abolition of Slavery. The son of a Maryland slave who had bought his freedom and a mother who had attained hers by escaping, he organized an orphanage for African-American children and founded the first Y.M.C.A. for his people. In his 14 years running a station in Philadelphia, Still conducted 649 "passengers" to freedom.

Still remained quietly in the background, depending on secrecy to carry on his work, but other Underground Railroad conductors became well known. The most famous was Harriet Tubman, an escaped slave who made more than 20 perilous trips back to the South and led over 300 men, women, and children to safety. Described as "strong as a man, brave as a lion, and cunning as a fox," Tubman was unable to read or write, but she tricked white authorities again and again. Slave owners, frantic to catch "the Black Moses," offered $40,000 for her capture, but she always made her escape, and she never lost a passenger. During the Civil War, Tubman served as a spy for the Union army. When she died in 1913, at the age of 87, she was buried with full military honors.

## John Brown

The courage of the abolitionists, black and white, stirred public feeling, but it was not enough for some. In 1858, a middle-aged white man named John Brown determined to take the ultimate step. He personally declared war on the slave states.

Brown was born in Connecticut in 1800—the year of Gabriel's revolt, Vesey's freedom, and Turner's birth—and studied briefly for the ministry. An unsuccessful tanner, wool dealer, cattle breeder, and farmer, he brooded about the injustice of slavery all his life. Brown was inspired by the heroism of Nat Turner and Cinqué. In 1855 he aided the escapes of several slaves and took his five sons to the Kansas Territory, which had just been opened for settlement, allowing the expansion of slavery. There he led a successful attack on proslavery forces. One of his sons lost his life in the battle.

Like Turner, Brown felt he had been called by God to root out the evil of slavery, and his magnetic personality drew others to him. With an "army" of five African Americans and 16 whites, he seized the federal armory in Harpers Ferry, Virginia (now West Virginia) on the night of October 16, 1859. By the next afternoon the Virginia militia and the U.S. Marines had the group surrounded. Brown was captured and ten of his men were killed, including two of his sons.

Brown was quickly tried, convicted of treason, and hanged. He calmly stated that he was as content "to die for God's eternal truth on the scaffold as in any other way." Like his hero Nat Turner, he had pleaded not guilty, arguing that he had acted in obedience to the will of a just God and felt no guilt. In fact, Brown declared during his trial, "I believe that to have interfered as I have done . . . in behalf of His despised poor, is no wrong, but right."

If Garrison seemed a fanatic, John Brown was considered a madman. But his action proved a turning point in the history of American slavery. His martyrdom was one of the many factors that triggered the Civil War. "God's angry man" became a symbol of justice, and Northern troops sang of him as they fought to save the Union. "John Brown's body lies a-mouldering in the grave," the song went, "His soul goes marching on."

## The Civil War and the End of Slavery

The outbreak of the Civil War in 1861 gave slaves a new means of resistance and free African Americans a direct way to support the abolitionist cause. The North resisted the idea of including "persons of African descent" in the army at first, but Secretary of War Edwin M. Stanton finally authorized the governor of Massachusetts to form the first black regiment in 1864. Frederick Douglass, the escaped slave who had written so powerfully of his life in bondage and was now an influential abolitionist, became a recruiter for the Union army, and two of his sons served in it. In time, some 180,000 African Americans fought with great valor in the Union army (under white officers) and 10,000 in the navy. They received $10 a month, $3 less than white soldiers and sailors. Thirty-eight thousand died in battle, and 21 received the Congressional Medal of Honor, America's highest military decoration.

In 1863, Lincoln issued an executive order liberating the slaves in rebel states "as a fit and necessary war measure." The Emancipation Proclamation did not free all the slaves in the country, and had no certainty of remaining in effect after the war, but it committed the government to a course of action. In 1865, with the war over and the defeated South too powerless to prevent it, a reunified nation passed the Thirteenth Amendment to the Constitution, guaranteeing that from that time forward "neither slavery nor involuntary servitude . . . shall exist within the United States."

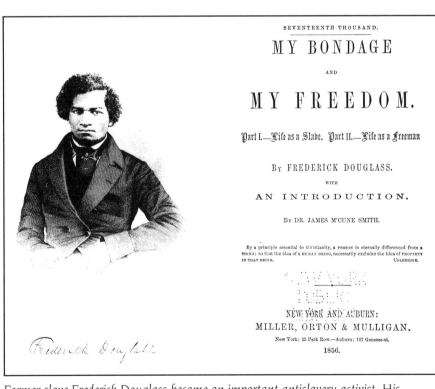

*Former slave Frederick Douglass became an important antislavery activist. His autobiography was among the most influential writings on the subject.* (New York Public Library, Schomburg Center for Research in Black Culture)

It had taken almost 300 years, and much more remained to be accomplished before complete justice would even be approached, but the dark shadow of slavery was lifted at last. The spirits of Gabriel and Denmark Vesey and Nat Turner and thousands of unnamed African sufferers were vindicated. Their seemingly doomed resistance had not been in vain.

## NOTES

p. 118   "Remember, Americans . . ." David Walker, *Walker's Appeal . . . to the Colored Citizens of the World, but in Particular, and Very Expressly to those of the United States of America* (1829; Salem N.H.: Ayer, 1994), p. 80.

p. 119   "I shall contend . . ." William Lloyd Garrison, *Liberator*, vol. I, no. 1, January 1, 1831.

p. 121   "In the name of the Merciful God . . ." Henry Highland Garnet, *An Address to the Slaves of the United States of America* (1843; Salem, N.H.: Ayer, 1994), pp. 95–96.

p. 126   "I believe that . . ." John Brown, October 31, 1859, quoted in John Anthony Scott, *Hard Trials on My Way* (New York: Alfred A. Knopf, 1974), p. 262.

# Bibliography

## General Histories of Slavery

Blassingame, John W. *The Slave Community: Plantation Life in the Antebellum South*. New York: Oxford University Press, 1972. Balanced examination of the slave experience.

Buckmaster, Henrietta. *Let My People Go: The Story of the Underground Railroad and the Growth of the Abolition Movement*. 1941. Columbia, S.C.: University of South Carolina Press, 1992. Pioneering history of the African-American struggle for freedom and justice.

Dillon, Merton. *Slavery Attacked: Southern Slaves and Their Allies, 1619–1865*. Baton Rouge, La.: Louisiana State University Press, 1990. Not always easy reading, but a clear and very thorough exploration of the battle against slavery in the United States.

Genovese, Eugene D. *The World the Slaveholders Made*. Middletown, Conn.: Wesleyan University Press, 1988. Critical examination of the thinking of slaveholders.

Harding, Vincent. *There Is a River: The Black Struggle for Freedom in America*. New York: Random House, 1981. Personal but extensively documented history with strong emotional impact.

Kolchin, Peter. *American Slavery: 1619–1877*. New York: Hill & Wang, 1993. Insightful examination of the subject giving a balanced view of both sides of the conflict.

Rawley, James A. *The Transatlantic Slave Trade*. New York: W. W. Norton, 1981. Complete discussion of the trade from the 16th to the 19th century.

Stampp, Kenneth M. *The Peculiar Institution: Slavery in the Ante-Bellum South*. 1956. New York: Vintage, 1989. Objective but compassionate examination of the history of slavery.

# Slave Rebellion

Aptheker, Herbert. *Negro Slave Revolts in the United States*. 1943. New York: International Publishers, 1993. Exhaustive report of organized rebellions from 1526 to 1860, citing about 250, treated in a sympathetic manner; somewhat controversial but generally accepted.

Carroll, Joseph Cephas. *Slave Insurrections in the United States, 1800–1865*. 1938. New York: Negro Universities Press, 1968. Even-handed and well-documented study; some of its details have been questioned by later historians.

Frey, Sylvia. *Water from the Rock: Black Resistance in a Revolutionary Age*. Princeton, N.J.: Princeton University Press, 1991. A clear examination of the African-American response to the Revolutionary War.

Halasz, Nicholas. *The Rattling Chains: Slave Unrest and Revolt in the Antebellum South*. New York: McKay, 1966. Stimulating examination of resistance from 1663 to the Civil War, outlining slavery's many abuses and considering the effects of slave rebellion on white racism.

Katz, William Loren. *Breaking the Chains: African-American Slave Resistance*. New York: Atheneum, 1990. Easy-to-read overview of the subject.

Mullin, Gerald. *Flight and Rebellion: Slave Resistance in Eighteenth-Century Virginia*. New York: Oxford University Press, 1972. History of the struggle against slavery from 1700 to 1800 in one colony; an important analysis, written at an advanced level.

# Slave Narratives

The best source of information on slave conditions is the reports of the slaves themselves. Many eloquent memoirs were written or dictated by former slaves during the 19th and early 20th centuries.

Bibb, Henry. *Narrative of the Life and Adventures of Henry Bibb, An American Slave*. 1850. Salem, N.H.: Ayer, 1991. Passionate attack on slavery recounting the life of one of its victims.

Blassingame, John W. *Slave Testimonies: Two Centuries of Letters, Speeches, Interviews, and Autobiographies.* Baton Rouge, La.: Louisiana University Press, 1978. Fascinating collection of firsthand reports of slave life.

Bontemps, Arna. *Five Black Lives.* Middletown, Conn.: Wesleyan University Press, 1971. Narratives of ex-slaves recalling experiences from 1729 to 1870.

Douglass, Frederick. *Narrative of the Life of Frederick Douglass, an American Slave.* 1845. Garden City, N.Y.: Doubleday, 1963.

——. *My Bondage and My Freedom.* 1855. New York: Arno Press, 1969.

——. *The Life and Times of Frederick Douglass, Written by Himself.* 1892. New York: Collier, 1962. Three versions of a moving personal story and a powerful indictment of the system.

Northrup, Solomon. *Twelve Years a Slave.* 1853. Baton Rouge, La.: Louisiana University Press, 1969. As exciting as a novel, the recollections of a freeman kidnapped into slavery.

Yetman, Norman. *Voices from Slavery.* New York: Holt, Rinehart, and Winston, 1970. Collection of slave reminiscences dictated during the 1930s, with interesting commentary.

## Gabriel

Bontemps, Arna. *Black Thunder: Gabriel's Revolt: Virginia: 1800.* 1936. Boston, Mass.: Beacon, 1968. Imaginative and often moving novel about Gabriel's heroic effort, rich in details of slave life.

Egerton, Douglas R. *Gabriel's Rebellion: The Virginia Slave Conspiracies of 1800 and 1802.* Chapel Hill, N.C.: University of North Carolina Press, 1993. Interesting reconstruction of the first major U.S. slave conspiracy and of another one inspired by it two years later, thoroughly researched and clearly written.

## Denmark Vesey

Lofton, John. *Denmark Vesey's Revolt: The Slave Plot That Lit a Fuse to Fort Sumter.* 1964. Kent, Ohio: Kent State University Press, 1983. Detailed social history that fills in the background of the Vesey revolt and argues that it led to the Civil War.

Starobin, Robert S. *Denmark Vesey: The Slave Conspiracy of 1822.* Englewood Cliffs, N.J.: Prentice-Hall, 1970. A complete collection of original source material about the plot.

# Nat Turner

Goldman, Marvin S. *Nat Turner and the Southampton Revolt of 1831.* New York: Franklin Watts, 1972. Popular account of the event, fills in the details of the background.

Oates, Stephen B. *The Fire of Jubilee: Nat Turner's Fierce Rebellion.* New York: Harper & Row, 1975. Exceptionally readable history based on sound scholarship.

Styron, William. *The Confessions of Nat Turner.* New York: Random House, 1966. Controversial and thought-provoking novelization of the life of Turner.

Tragle, Henry Irving. *The Southampton Slave Revolt of 1831: A Compilation of Source Material.* Amherst, Mass.: University of Massachusetts Press, 1971. The definitive collection of original documents, including the text of Turner's *Confessions.*

# Cinqué and the Amistad

Jones, Howard. *Mutiny on the Amistad: The Saga of a Slave Revolt and Its Impact on American Abolition, Law, and Diplomacy.* New York: Oxford University Press, 1987. Stirring, clearly written account of the event and its effects on U.S. slavery and international relations.

# Haiti and the Caribbean

Hunt, Alfred N. *Haiti's Influence on Antebellum America: Slumbering Volcano in the Caribbean.* Baton Rouge, La.: Louisiana University Press, 1988. Thorough study of the slave revolt with special emphasis on how it affected U.S. slaves and abolitionists.

Parkinson, Wenda. *'This Gilded African': Toussaint L'Ouverture.* London: Quartet Books, 1978. Comprehensive account of "the first black freedom fighter," stresses his courage and vision.

Vandercook, John W. *Black Majesty: The Life of Christophe, King of Haiti.* 1928. Garden City, N.Y.: Garden City Publishing, 1950. Dramatic retelling of Henri Christophe's life, providing the history of his times in vivid detail.

# Index

Boldface numbers indicate major topics.
*Italic* numbers indicate illustrations.
Numbers followed by *m* indicate maps.

## B

## C

## D

## E

Emancipation Proclamation   127
Emerson, Ralph Waldo   83

## F

Ferrer, Ramon   102, 108, 111
Fitzhugh, George   4, 23
Franklin, Benjamin   20
French Revolution   48, 60, 61, 62
Fugitive Slave Laws (1793, 1850)   41, **82–83**, 123

## G

Gabriel   **49–58**, 72, 73, 77, 81, 82, 83, 85, 89, 90, 102, 115, 117,
   118, 125, 128
Garnet, Henry Highland   **121–122**
Garrison, William Lloyd   **119–120**, *120*, 121, 123
Gedney, Lt.   106
Gell, Monday   80, 84
Grey, Thomas R.   94, 96
Gullah, Jack   80

## H

Haiti   *See* Saint-Domingue
Hamnett, Bacchus   81
Harpers Ferry, Va.   125
Harth, Minto   80
Helper, Hinton Rowan   86

## J

Jackson, Andrew   4
Jamaica   **68–70**, 73, 74, 102
Jamestown Colony   9, 16
Jefferson, Thomas   20, 48, 50, **54–55**, 56, 57, 97, 110

Ozanne, T. D. 35

## P

Poyas, Peter 84, 85
Plato 5
Prosser, Thomas H. 49–50, 54

## Q

Quaker 52, 57, 117, 123

## R

Randolph, John 53
Rolla 80, 82, 84
Ruiz, Jose 102, 103, 105, 106
Saffin, John 5
Saint-Dominque (Haiti) 48, **61–68**, 73, 74, 79, 80, 83, 85, 86, 102, 113
Salem, Peter 43
Sancho (Gabriel recruiter) 57
Seabrook, Whitemarsh B. 70
Sheffey, Daniel 73
Sheppard, Mosby 49, 50, 54
slavery
  in antiquity **2–4**
  in the Middle Ages **5–6**
  in Africa **6–7**
  defense of 1, **4–5**
  of native peoples 7, 8, 9, 16
  laws against 20
Smith, Peter 53
Spartacus 3–4, 70
Stanton, Edwin M. 126
Still, William 124
Stono, S.C., rebellion (1739) **44**, 48
Stowe, Harriet Beecher **123–124**